CLICK

Ori Brafman is an organizational business consultant, and the coauthor of the *New York Times* bestseller *Sway* and the critically acclaimed book *The Starfish and the Spider*. He lectures internationally in front of Fortune 500, government and military audiences. He holds an MBA from Stanford Graduate School of Business.

Rom Brafman is a psychologist with a private practice in Palo Alto, California and the coauthor of *Sway*. He has won awards for excellence in teaching and promoting positive human growth.

They both in live in the San Francisco Bay Area.

Also by Ori Brafman and Rom Brafman

Sway

By Ori Brafman

The Starfish and the Spider (coauthor)

CLICK

The Magic of Instant Connections

– and how they can transform our work and relationships

ORI BRAFMAN
AND
ROM BRAFMAN

2 4 6 8 10 9 7 5 3

Published in 2010 by Virgin Books, an imprint of Ebury Publishing
A Random House Group Company

First published in the United States by Broadway Books, an imprint of the
Crown Publishing Group, a division of Random House, Inc., New York

The Random House Group Limited Reg. No. 954009

Addresses for companies within the Random House Group can be found at
www.randomhouse.co.uk

A CIP catalogue record for this book is available from the British Library

The Random House Group Limited supports The Forest Stewardship
Council [FSC], the leading international forest certification organisation.
All our titles that are printed on Greenpeace-approved FSC-certified paper
carry the FSC logo. Our paper procurement policy can be found at:
www.rbooks.co.uk/environment

Mixed Sources
Product group from well-managed
forests and other controlled sources
www.fsc.org Cert no. TT-COC-2139
© 1996 Forest Stewardship Council
FSC

Design by Leonard W. Henderson

Printed and bound in Great Britain by Clays Ltd, St Ives PLC

ISBN 9780753539392

To buy books by your favourite authors and register for offers visit:
www.rbooks.co.uk/environment

For John Buckley Roberts,
in loving memory

CONTENTS

CHAPTER 1

Finding Magic

Sitting by the pool at a Pasadena hotel, Paul was about to do something impulsive, even by his standards.

The Southern California evening breeze was starting to pick up. Anyone within earshot of Paul and the woman sitting across from him at the poolside table would have thought they'd known each other for years, although the pair had met only two days prior. They talked about everything from world travel to the 1970s antiwar movement to Socratic philosophy; their conversation had a casual, easy flow to it. Watching the two of them—Nadia with her fine Mediterranean features and striking jet-black hair and Paul with his rugged, all-American looks—one had a sense that they fit together. It was as if each was attuned to what the other was thinking. One moment they were laughing at embarrassing childhood stories and the next they were finishing each other's sentences. If there's such a thing as synergy between two people, it seemed almost palpable here.

One would never have suspected that the two were ostensibly meeting for work. At the time, Paul was in charge of the proposal for a $15 billion project to clean up a nuclear weapons facility in Colorado. To help put the proposal together, Paul had assembled experts from around the world. The team had taken over an office building in Pasadena; the work was so intense that the office remained open 24/7. It was Paul's role to make sure all the countless moving parts worked together. But he was used to this level of intensity. A former officer in the army's special forces, Paul was trained to make split-second decisions, and he has the kind of personality people instinctively respond to—he is a natural leader. In conversation, he focuses intently on the other person's every word, making it clear he's fully present and is listening carefully.

Every morning at exactly 8:15 a.m., Paul assembled the top executives from the team to brief them about the strategy for the day. The meeting several days ago, though, had been different. From the beginning, Paul was keenly aware of the new team member, Nadia. "I immediately thought, *Who is that?*" He found himself instantly attracted to her. Nadia's initial reaction to Paul seemed to be very different, however. It was her first day on the job. Her vacation in Paris had been abruptly cut short so that she could fly to Pasadena and take over as the project's chief operating officer. If that hadn't soured her mood enough, Paul made a comment during the meeting—seemingly out of left field—that soured it further.

"I uttered something about there being nothing new in human relations since the time of Plato, Aristotle, and Socrates," he recalled. "I don't even remember why."

A few minutes later, as Paul stood before the group, he noticed out of the corner of his eye a folded note being passed from person to person. As he continued speaking, the note eventually made its way to him. He unfolded it and read the first line: "I completely disagree with you." The hand-scrawled note went on for an entire page. But it was unsigned. He looked up, searching for a nod from the note's author. But all he got were blank stares. Only after the meeting had ended and the rest of his staff had filed out of the room did Nadia walk up to Paul.

Remembers Nadia, "Here we haven't met yet, and I just wrote him a note that said, 'I don't agree with you; what about the change in master-slave relations and relationships between men and women? There have been so many advances in society since then. How can you make such a comment? I'd like to discuss this with you.'"

Paul, instead of becoming defensive, was intrigued. "I'd like to continue the conversation with you," he told her.

"Anytime," she fired back.

Twelve hours later they were sitting by the pool.

They had told themselves that they intended to use the time not just to resolve the argument but also to delve into some important work issues. Work, however, never came up during their conversation together. Toward the end of the evening, the intensity of their interaction was difficult to ignore.

"Are we going to end up getting in trouble?" Paul asked Nadia, realizing that they were letting work get away from them.

"Yes," she said simply. It was clear to her from the beginning that there was something special between them. "The moment he made that comment about Plato and Aristotle," she told us, "I knew. What we valued in life was very much the same, as were the things we thought were trivial. Who's outrageous enough to even bring up Plato and Aristotle in the middle of a strategy session? I mean, what does anybody who's in there know about Plato and the Greeks, or care about them? He had that courage to be different."

Having accomplished little of the work they had been planning to do, the pair decided to meet again the following night by the pool. And it was then that it happened. Paul looked at Nadia and asked, "What would you say if I told you that I loved you and wanted to marry you?"

Nadia retorted, "Is that a hypothetical or is that an offer?"

Paul said, "Let's see what tomorrow brings."

Let's hit the pause button here. First, it's worth noting that Paul and Nadia weren't teenagers driven by hyperactive hormones. They were seasoned business executives. Like most of us, when they met a new person, they usually spent their first moments sizing each other up, searching for something to talk about: *Where are you from? What kind of work do you do?*

Occasionally, though, an introduction to someone new is more intense and intimate from the get-go. Maybe we share the same sense of humor or we admire the other individual's personality or passion. Or we immediately sense that we can just be ourselves around that person. Things feel right; we hit it off. There is an immediate sense of familiarity and comfort. Conversation flows easily, without embarrassing pauses or self-consciousness. In essence, we click.

This book is about those mysterious moments—when we click in life. Those moments when we are fully engaged and feel a certain natural chemistry or connection with a person, place, or activity.

In its simplest terms, clicking can be defined as an immediate, deep, and meaningful connection with another person or with the world around us. Typically, it takes weeks or months before most of us feel truly comfortable with a new person. We have to gain the other person's trust, and he or she needs to gain ours. We need to find a common language, understand each other's quirks, and establish an emotional bond. But sometimes this process is greatly accelerated, and the connection seems to form almost magically and instantaneously.

But this type of immediate, deep connection isn't limited to romantic love. Clicking can be equally deep and meaningful between future friends and can strike in the most unlikely of places.

For Jim West and Gerhard Sessler, a pair of physicists who first met at Bell Laboratories, the instant connection between them would permanently alter the course of their careers. But if you were to go back to 1959 and see the two when they first met, you'd be struck by their apparent differences.

Jim, a tall, slender African American who grew up in Virginia during the Great Depression, learned from an early age to make do with whatever resources were available to him. "As a black man," he reflected, "I attended segregated schools. But I was lucky in that I had great teachers."

These teachers—along with his family, friends, and neighbors—saw something special in the boy. As his brother tells it, Jim was the kind of kid who always had a screwdriver or tool of some sort in his hand. When he wasn't taking apart his grandfather's watch, he was rebuilding an old vacuum-tube radio. As a teenager, Jim decided to channel his love of tinkering into a career in physics. Concerned, his father introduced him to three black men who held Ph.D.'s in physics or chemistry. Recalls Jim, "The best jobs they could find were at the post office. [The point my father was making was that] I was taking the long road toward working at the post office."

Jim persevered nonetheless, eventually landing a job at Bell Laboratories. It was the equivalent, for an engineer, of working at Disneyland. "It was the premier research institute in the country," Jim explains. "People from all over the world wanted to work there."

His first day at Bell Labs, Jim was assigned an office next door to another new recruit, Gerhard Sessler. Sporting short-cropped hair and a fastidious wardrobe, Gerhard had a natural, genteel warmth about him. While Jim had been raised in the American South, Gerhard had grown up in pre–World War II Germany. "I was only eight years old when the war started," recalls Gerhard. "The air raids, the atmosphere—it was a very difficult time."

It was very unusual in 1959 for an African American man from the South to be working side by side with a German immigrant. But the two immediately hit it off. Even though Gerhard's thick German accent was difficult for Jim's American ears to understand, from the beginning the pair launched into long discussions about physics and life. As Gerhard tells it, "From the start, I noticed Jim was intellectually curious and sharp—always exploring new things. I was immediately drawn to that."

"We were both new," recalls Jim, "and being a member of an underrepresented minority, it was unusually lonely. But with Gerhard, I knew I could always be myself. I think it's fair to say that we clicked right off the bat."

The two spent hours discussing science and theories of the natural world, and the more they talked, the more intense the interaction became. In the course of one of these impassioned conversations, the two came up with an

ingenious idea, one that would lead to one of the great-
est achievements in acoustics history: the invention of the
modern microphone.

Comparing Jim and Gerhard's story with Paul and
Nadia's, we see two very different types of relationships
emerging. But if we take a close look at the two budding
relationships, we see that they follow a similar trajectory.
Both began with what we call *quick-set intimacy*. In other
contexts, the words *quick* and *instant* don't necessarily
sound like positive descriptions (think instant coffee or
quick TV dinners). But when it comes to human relationships, the bonds formed by quick-set intimacy can be surprisingly strong and create a tenor in the relationship that
may be lifelong. In our exploration of clicking, we'll investigate the different factors that go into forming quick-set
intimacy. What happens in that moment when we first
sense our interest in another person? Why do we click with
some people and not with others? Why do those moments
make us feel more fully connected not just to that individual but to everything around us? Is there a way to foster or
proactively create that kind of instant intimacy?

When we click in a relationship—whether the relationship is a romantic one or involves meeting a new friend at
a party or forging a special connection with a teammate
or colleague—we are affected in several significant ways.
First, clicking brings about a unique, almost euphoric
state, one that we describe as "magical." Second, it perma-

nently alters the fundamental nature of the relationship. And last, it can serve to elevate our own personal abilities.

Let's look at what actually happens when quick-set intimacy takes place. Paul remembers that the moment he met Nadia, he felt an overwhelming attraction to her. Nadia puts it slightly differently. She felt an instant sense of comfort and a surprising intensity of feeling: "The attraction was just magical." And neither Paul nor Nadia uses words such as *magical* loosely—Paul was a former military officer, you'll recall, and Nadia was a senior manager with a degree in nuclear engineering.

The two physicists at Bell Labs expressed a similar intensity. "Somehow, from the very, very start," reflects Gerhard, "there was always sympathy for the other person. There was always an understanding. We had such an appreciation for each other."

Most of us have had that feeling of magic at some time in our lives. But it can be difficult to articulate. The next time you encounter someone whom you instantly, magically hit it off with, pay attention to what you are experiencing in that moment. There's a certain quality of infatuation; it is exciting, even thrilling. We often feel more alive, more engaged, more *there*. We're more in touch with the other person, or with our surroundings, and with ourselves.

Neuroscientists decided to try to take a peek into the biology behind clicking in a romantic context. The researchers scoured the community for individuals who identified themselves as being "madly in love." When they placed these people in a functional magnetic resonance imaging (fMRI) machine to scan their brains, they observed that the parts of their brains responsible for dopamine absorption were extraordinarily active—so much so that the individuals almost looked like they were under the influence of narcotics. Dopamine is the chemical that fuels the brain's pleasure center, producing the kind of euphoria we associate with feeling fully alive. This is a noticeable and significant high—and from a strictly biological perspective, it has an allure not unlike that of such drugs as cocaine, nicotine, and amphetamines.

Every time we feel that sense of being fully engaged and alive, whether as a result of a connection with another person, an activity such as sports—being "in the zone"—or simply feeling at one with the world around us, we experience a surge of dopamine through our brain. The magnitude of the chemical reward we get when we make these intimate connections stands in stark contrast to our complete lack of such a reward when we are feeling socially disconnected. To study this effect, a team of neuroscientists from UCLA and Australia placed participants in fMRI machines and asked them to play a virtual ball-tossing game. In the game, participants were under the impression that they were playing electronic catch with other participants in the room. But in reality they were just playing with a computer. After a few rounds, the computer deliberately ignored the participants by no longer tossing the ball to them. If being madly in love floods the brain with dopamine, feeling cut off and alone—even in the course of a simple game of virtual catch—lit up the anterior cingulate cortex, the part of the brain associated with physical pain.

Why does the brain go to such extremes to reward us for connecting or fully engaging with the world around us and to punish us for feeling cut off and alone? To solve this mystery, we must turn to behavioral psychology. But we immediately encounter an unexpected hurdle. Traditionally, research psychologists have spent very little time trying to understand *positive* human emotions, let alone the magic of clicking. There's plenty of research explaining why people get divorced or why they feel depressed—a wealth of data about the difficult moments in our lives. But there's surprisingly little about our best moments. Those isolated studies having to do with positive emotions (such as happiness and optimism) tend to deal with them in the context of getting by in difficult situations, or preventing one from falling into a depressed state, or recovering from a traumatic experience.

In a very real way, psychologists' emphasis on pathology limits us to seeing only one side of the human equation. As a psychologist himself, Rom believes that previously unexplored aspects of positive emotions would illuminate just as much about human nature as do their negative counterparts: Why is it that we form close, meaningful connections? What happens to us emotionally and psychologically when we do? And why does such an experience often feel so intense and pleasurable?

To answer these questions, Rom examined the formation of such magical moments. He knew he was venturing outside the traditional realm of academic inquiry, but he was convinced that this was a significant and powerful part of the human experience about which we understood very little.

Rom asked a diverse set of participants—psychology majors, football players, fraternity brothers, and so on—to recount a special or exciting experience in their lives that they felt had a magical quality: "a unique moment or event that was for you filled with magic." Surprisingly, every single participant was able to conjure a magical experience from his or her life. The stories were as varied and diverse as the individuals in the room. An overwhelming majority of the recollections involved a sense of connection, of clicking.

One participant described the immediate sense of intimacy she'd felt when she met her future boyfriend: "From the moment we both looked into each other's eyes we knew there was something special there. The whole night felt like a dream." Another subject, a young man, recalled rekindling the special bond with his mother: "It was the first time I said 'I love you' to my mother as an adult. She was telling me about the things that happened to her in her life and I was telling her about things in my life. That was a beautiful day." Another woman recalled an experience she had as a teenager: "My first kiss. It was with my first boyfriend and longtime best friend. It was tingly/sweet/sincere/romantic. It made my birthday magical."

There are two points that are worth noting here. First, all the individuals described these magical moments of connection using nearly identical words: *euphoric, energizing, thrilling,* and *special.* In fact, looking at just the emotions associated with the experience, you wouldn't know whether the participant was describing a marriage proposal or a hike with friends. And that is part of the point. Although the individuals had very different experiences and arrived at this magical moment in different ways, they experienced it *identically.*

Second, when we subsequently asked a different set of people to describe "a time in your life when you clicked" with another person—as opposed to experienced a "magical moment"—they used exactly the same emotional descriptors as the participants did in the earlier study. In terms of the emotions they engender, quick-set intimacy and magical experiences appear inextricably linked.

Now, think about the fMRI studies about emotional connections and biological rewards. When we click with someone, when we get that surge of dopamine running through our neurons, we're tapping into the very same place that we tap into when we experience a magical moment. That is one of the reasons the experience is so meaningful and powerful.

In the course of *Click,* we'll explore our hardwired tendency to connect with other people and experience meaningful events. We'll look at the specific factors that turn ordinary moments of emotional connection into magical ones. For now, though, it's enough to recognize that quick-set intimacy starts a chain reaction in our brains that fundamentally changes the nature of our relationship with the person, place, or activity.

Let's return to Pasadena and Paul and Nadia as they sit by the pool. Their second evening together, Paul hinted that he was falling in love with Nadia, even though they had just met. On their third night together, he asked her to marry him. And Nadia, just as caught up in the emotion, accepted. They felt like they were being swept up by a force that was bigger than either of them. A month later, the two were married.

Given how quickly they were engaged and married, did their relationship last?

It has. "That same magic we had in Pasadena," reflected Paul, "is still at the heart of our relationship." In other words, the experience of clicking can remain a permanent part of a relationship.

For Jim and Gerhard, the way the two of them clicked manifested itself as an intense closeness; it was as if they were in their own world. Remembers Gerhard: "When we were together, we were operating on a different level. We found ourselves more willing to pursue new angles and theories." Their passion for ideas and high regard for each other, he explains, were always present.

"One time," recalls Gerhard, "we were contacted by the Philharmonic Hall of Lincoln Center in New York. They built a new fancy concert hall, but the acoustics inside were very poor. The music critics wrote about it in the newspapers; it was a big embarrassment. Our job was to figure out why the acoustics were so poor and why the sound reverberated unevenly."

The solution to this problem proved more challenging than the two initially had expected. "To figure out what was going on, you had to fill the room with sound," remembers Jim. "And you had to do it in a very short burst. Most of the environments that we had interrogated up to that point were much smaller and we were able to use something like a starter pistol to excite the enclosure. But the concert hall was far too big for that."

"Of course we had loudspeakers," interjects Gerhard. "But we needed a big bang, so to speak. We spent a lot of time brainstorming for solutions, and finally Jim said, 'Hey, I have an idea.'"

"I'd been to football games down at Rutgers," Jim explained, "and I'd seen that little cannon that they rolled out during the game. They only shot it when Rutgers scored a touchdown, and it wasn't exactly the best team at the time, so they didn't shoot it much." He realized, "'That makes a lot of noise; let me try that.' I talked to the athletics department and asked to borrow it. I had to sign my life away, but they let me use it."

Imagine two distinguished scientists rolling a cannon into Lincoln Center. Says Gerhard, "Jim prepared everything, and when it was all ready to go, he fired the cannon." The acoustic burst was exactly what they'd hoped for: a really big explosion of sound. But they got more than they bargained for. "The manager ran in when he heard the bang, and he wasn't sure what was happening. He said, 'What's going on here?' The hall was full of smoke. He gasped, 'Oh, gosh! We have a concert tonight. How are we going to get the smoke out of this room?'" It took three or four days to clear out the smoke, remembers Jim. But smoke and all, Jim and Gerhard's cannon blast revealed a small area near the ceiling that was responsible for the acoustic abnormalities.

You need a certain level of creativity, along with a sense of chutzpah, to pull off something like that. It was another quality Jim and Gerhard shared.

But can the success of Jim and Gerhard's relationship be attributed to the nature of their initial connection? Would Jim and Gerhard have formed the same kind of relationship, with the same shared passion and durability, if they hadn't clicked in the first place?

In the Netherlands, a husband-and-wife psychology team, Dick Barelds and Pieternel Barelds-Dijkstra, set out to better understand the effects of clicking and quick-set intimacy on long-term relationships. Rather than focusing on dopamine levels, the Bareldses were interested in how an instant bond of this nature affected the relationship years after that initial spark.

The Bareldses contacted one thousand couples whom they randomly selected from the Dutch phone book. Each couple was invited to take a survey that explored the fundamental health of their relationship. Because the questions were personal and revealing, husbands and wives took the surveys separately. They were assured that their responses would remain strictly confidential. This allowed the Bareldses to ask rather probing personal questions of the couples—and gain unusual insight into their marriages.

Their responses revealed that the couples tended to fall into one of three categories. The first were those who'd been longtime friends before they started dating. These couples had known each other very well; eventually, over time, the relationship had turned from a platonic one into a romantic one.

The second group had followed a traditional courtship— the couples went on numerous dates, gradually became more serious and intimate, and eventually decided to get married.

The last group started out as strangers and—like Paul and Nadia—immediately clicked and fell headlong in love.

After an average of twenty-five years together, all three groups—at least on the surface—looked similar: They had similar levels of education, similar household incomes, and an average of 2.1 kids. And when you looked at their individual personality traits, there were no significant differences among the groups.

But the Bareldses wondered if there were significant differences that would emerge when they examined the underlying quality of the couples' relationships. The Bareldses predicted that the couples who had been friends first and those who had dated for a substantial amount of time would enjoy higher-quality relationships than their counterparts who had fallen in love in an instant. They reasoned that if you take your time to really get to know the other person, you're more likely to end up with a spouse who's compatible with and similar to you, making for a better long-term match.

And indeed, the data showed that those couples who had been friends first and those who had dated extensively were more similar to one another than those who had clicked. But when the Bareldses asked the couples to evaluate themselves with regard to statements having to do with commitment and closeness (e.g., "I could not let anything get in the way of my commitment to [my spouse]"; "I expect my love for [my spouse] to last for the rest of my life"; "I value [my spouse] greatly in my life"; "I feel that [my spouse] really understands me"), there was virtually no difference among the groups.

Some individual relationships were closer and more committed than others, but regardless of how the couples began their relationship, all three groups scored about the same in terms of commitment and closeness. In other words, although the spouses in the friends-first couples and the dating couples shared more similarity than those who had fallen in love at first sight, the quality of the relationships in all the groups was equal.

While similarity is indeed important in a strong, lasting relationship, when the Bareldses asked additional questions that were even more revealing and intimate, they discovered another, equally powerful factor that contributed to the health of the relationships of those who had fallen headlong in love. They asked the couples how they would respond to each of the following statements: "There is something almost 'magical' about my relationship with [my spouse]"; "When I see romantic movies and read romantic books I think of [my spouse]"; "I find myself thinking about [my spouse] frequently during the day"; "I cannot imagine another person making me as happy as [my spouse] does"; "I melt when looking deeply into [my spouse's] eyes." These statements describe an ongoing level of intensity, even years later, that is uncommon among couples. How many of us melt, after all, when we look at our spouse?

When the Bareldses analyzed the results from this section of the survey, they found that, as a group, those who had clicked were more likely than their counterparts to agree with these statements. These people spent more time thinking about their spouses, found it difficult to imagine being married to anyone else, and felt that there was a magic to the relationship. In other words, they were significantly more likely to exhibit a higher level of passion in their relationships, even after marriage, kids, and the mortgage.

It's important to remember that those individuals who had clicked with their future spouse weren't any different from the other individuals in terms of personality. It wasn't that they were naturally more passionate. Instead, *because* they clicked, whatever the couples lacked in commonality they made up for in mutual passion. And that directly translated into a high-quality relationship.

When Rom analyzed the results of his study on magical moments, he found that simply recalling magical moments, even years later, produced nearly identical levels of passion and intensity as the original experience. You might expect that with the passage of time people's memories would fade and the emotions would lose their power. But as the subjects recalled their magical moment during the study, they experienced the feeling of magic all over again. More than 90 percent of the respondents said they felt happy and excited and even reported reliving the original intensity: "It makes me smile," said one. "It brings me so much happiness and joy," said another. "I get such a wonderful feeling inside recalling the magic I felt that day." One participant remarked that it was "almost like I'm back there; I wish I was." Another said, "It fills me again with what I felt that night—puts me back into that frame of mind, calms me." Yet another participant reported, "It stirs the same feeling from when I first realized I was in love. It's magical all over again."

What the couples in the Bareldses' study were articulating is something that we came to realize is an important principle of clicking: that the magic of quick-set intimacy continues to define the tenor of the relationship even years later.

Similarly, fifty years after they first met, Bell Lab physicists Gerhard Sessler and Jim West describe the intensity of their partnership in the same way. "There was a certain ethereal quality to our collaboration when we began, and it continued to be there even when I retired," recalls Gerhard. "I've worked with many people in my life, but the relationship with Jim was the best."

This special type of bond doesn't only alter the quality of the relationship—it can also serve to bring out the best in the abilities and attributes of those involved. For Jim and Gerhard it resulted in their being able to solve a tricky problem that had vexed audio engineers for decades.

In one of their early conversations together at Bell Labs, Jim and Gerhard started talking about microphones. The instruments used at the time were quite bulky (think of a 1950s radio announcer shouting into a big metal grille) because they relied on an external power source. This limited the wide-scale application of microphones, especially in compact and mobile devices.

"The microphone consisted of small carbon granules with an external source," explains Gerhard. "It was a crazy, outdated type of device, but it worked. People at Bell Labs told us, 'You can never beat this.'" After months of back-and-forth conversation about how to improve the device, Jim and Gerhard hit upon a simple yet ingenious solution: why not insert an electric power source (an electret, composed of a charged foil) directly into the microphone? With no reliance on external power, you could create a much smaller device.

From the get-go, Jim and Gerhard ran into resistance. Bell Labs questioned why two of its most promising scientists would occupy themselves with a seemingly impossible problem. They received a great deal of pressure to abandon the project. Time and again, the pair supported each other despite the naysayers. "Look, if I had to do it alone," explains Gerhard, "if I didn't have Jim there, I would have given up a long time ago." They relied on their bond to keep them charging ahead. In a very real way, quick-set intimacy can help to bring out the best in us, especially in facing challenges. "That same spark that initially drew us together kept us going even when everyone told us to abandon the project," Gerhard said. Their passion and drive were unwavering.

Today, the product of Jim and Gerhard's collaboration accounts for the vast majority of all microphones produced. Every time you use your cell phone, camcorder, or laptop, you're benefiting from the invention that they came up with because they clicked together so long ago.

As for Paul and Nadia, fifteen years after they first met,

it's clear that the magic of their initial encounter still plays a key role in their relationship. Today the couple runs an emergency management company called ESi. "It wasn't easy that first year," Nadia confides. "We've had our challenges." Nor are the two of them always on the same page. But they're never afraid to disagree. As Nadia explains, "I wouldn't have it any other way. If either one of us would cave in, it would be detrimental to our decision-making process. We absolutely need to evaluate everything from different perspectives. That's what makes us powerful." She pauses and smiles. "About the only thing that we've always agreed on is how important we are in each other's lives." That initial spark has had a lasting effect on their relationship. It's clear that these types of interactions aren't just ephemeral occurrences.

But *why* do we click in the first place? What are the hidden forces working to make those connections occur? To examine the first of what we call *click accelerators*, we visit a police officer embroiled in a hostage situation, where the magic of an instant connection can be the difference between life and death.

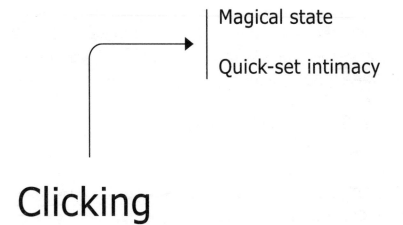

Magical state

Quick-set intimacy

Clicking

CHAPTER 2

The Vulnerable Hostage Negotiator and the Click Accelerators

P olice officer Greg Sancier raced through traffic, keenly aware that every minute mattered. The crisis intervention specialist had just been notified that a man had broken into a house in San Jose, California, and was holding the inhabitants hostage at gunpoint. It was Sancier's job to ensure that everyone got out alive.

"The minute I leave my house," he said, "I know that I will have to be there five, ten, fifteen hours straight. Every time I go out, I say a prayer: 'God, please give me the strength to do what I need to do tonight to help save people's lives.' Because sometimes I don't know how I'm going to get them out, to be honest."

Sancier—a twenty-five-year veteran of the force—draws upon his extensive training in human behavior when dealing with these crisis situations. He is one of only a few hostage negotiators in the country who holds a Ph.D. in psychology.

Square-faced, solidly built, and broad-shouldered, Sancier has the look of a former college athlete. He is outgoing and friendly—even gregarious, some might say—and quick to flash a smile behind his mustache. His warm, easygoing manner is more reminiscent of someone hanging out with a buddy at a barbecue than of a hostage negotiator in a high-pressure situation. It's this very quality that makes Sancier so successful in crisis situations.

Sancier's approach to negotiations offers an important perspective on how instant connections are made. When most of us think about how or why we click with another person, we usually do so in our mental rearview mirror, reflecting on an isolated, serendipitous occasion when we formed a powerful connection. Sancier is able to *create* that kind of instant intimacy on demand, even under the most stressful of conditions. In other words, instant intimacy isn't necessarily serendipitous; it doesn't always occur by happenstance.

So what is it that can help someone to form that kind of instant connection?

As Sancier drove to the scene, he began to mull over the challenge facing him. The hostage taker, a man by the name of Ed Jones, was what is called a "three-striker" in California: Jones had already been convicted of two violent felonies, and if charged with a third, he faced a mandatory life sentence under California law. Jones knew this as well: "He wasn't going to go to prison without killing himself or killing someone else," Sancier told us later. "He was a gang member; to achieve status within gangs, you want to go out in a blaze of glory. You might have heard of the term 'suicide by cop.' He was going to force our hand so we'd kill him."

Despite the tactical skills of the officers on the scene and the immense firepower at their disposal, the only feasible way of guaranteeing that the situation would be resolved without loss of either the hostages' lives or Jones's was to convince Jones to give himself up. And to do that, Sancier knew, he had to form some kind of connection with Jones.

As it turns out, Sancier's ability to build instant connections with hostage takers has important implications for us in our everyday interactions. Sancier arrives at a crime scene with a metaphorical toolbox. It contains different approaches to establishing rapport, and he uses whatever tool he needs to get the job done. "Whatever I can hang my hat on, if you will, that's what I grab," he explained. "If it's relating to the suspect man to man, fine. If it's that we both like fishing, fine. Whatever it is."

For Sancier, there's an art to establishing a relationship in this kind of high-pressure situation. He draws upon his natural charm, likability, and friendliness to reach out to such suspects. But alongside the art, there's also some interesting science. Recent research has identified subtle yet powerful psychological cues that can help to create a click. Even seemingly small gestures or actions and expressions can make a significant difference.

In one study, individuals were brought into a room and introduced to someone they had never met before. Each pair was then presented with ethical dilemmas (e.g., "What would you do if you saw your friend's fiancé kissing someone else?" or "What would you do if you saw your sibling steal something valuable?"). The pair had to debate and attempt to resolve these quandaries, which had no single clear answer.

What the participants didn't realize was that the researchers didn't really care about the teams' responses. Unbeknownst to the participants, their assigned partners were actually research assistants whose task was to gauge the effect of subtle physical touch on personal attraction.

With half the participants, the research assistant simply played along and discussed the ethical problems. But with the other half, the assistant casually touched the participant three times during the course of the five-minute conversation: once on the shoulder and twice on the elbow. The participants, busy reflecting on the moral dilemmas, hardly noticed the casual touches, or at most gave their partner a brief sideways glance.

These seemingly innocuous casual touches, however, turned out to have a much bigger impact than anyone would have guessed. At the end of the interactions, the researchers surveyed the participants and asked them what they thought about their partners. It turned out that those individuals who were touched by their partner were far more likely to feel a sense of connection. They reported feeling greater "immediacy, affection, receptivity, trust, relaxation, similarity, and informality" with their partner.

Because we unconsciously associate touch with closeness, being touched, even for a second, makes us far more attracted to the person touching us. It makes us more prone to form a connection. A similar pattern emerges with casual eye contact. During a job interview, for instance, candidates who maintain eye contact are far more likely to establish rapport with their interviewers. They've been found to form a closer relationship and are typically judged by the interviewer to be a better fit for the position (regardless of their actual job skill level).

Touching or looking at someone is an immediate indicator that we like him or her—it's a natural way of communicating closeness or affection. What's interesting is that the recipient not only picks up on these cues but unconsciously reciprocates the perceived affection. When we get cues that we're liked, we're automatically drawn to like the other person in return.

Other senses, too, can play a role in creating an instant connection. Scientists have begun to explore the roles played by smell and pheromones—chemicals given off by animals that can help to foster attraction. Scientists long believed that humans, unlike other animal species, do not manufacture or respond to pheromones. But many couples claim there *is* something about the scent of their partner that is special, distinctive, and attractive.

Is there any truth to these sentiments? To find out, researchers showed two different groups of women a stack of pictures of men whom they hadn't previously met. The first group of women, after taking a good look at the photos, were asked to evaluate the men on several aspects of attractiveness: general looks, body attractiveness, self-assuredness, intelligence, and relationship-worthiness. The second group of women were shown identical pictures of the men and were asked to perform the same task as the first group. But atop a shelf in the office where they were sitting, the researchers had placed small cotton pads that had been worn by a different group of men under their armpits for eight hours. The odor from these "auxiliary extracts" was far too weak to be consciously picked up by any of the women. And at first the presence of the pads didn't seem to have any noticeable effect. Both groups of women—those who were exposed to the scents and those who weren't—rated the men equally when it came to qualities that spoke to long-term relationship potential (e.g., good with kids, intelligent, or relationship-worthy). But a surprising difference emerged when the researchers examined indicators of the women's more immediate, raw attraction. The group who had been exposed to the cotton pads rated the men in the pictures as having sexier bodies, more striking facial features, and more self-assurance than did the group of women who hadn't been exposed to the pads. The least attractive men, in particular, enjoyed the biggest bump in ratings compared with the control group.

Apparently, the neocortex of the women—the relatively

modern part of the brain in charge of executive decision making, such as long-term mate selection—was unfazed by exposure to the subtle odors. But the primitive brain was powerfully affected. Without their realizing it, the scent from the cotton pads bypassed the women's higher cognitive functions and directly affected their base, physical attraction to the men in the pictures.

What scientists now realize is that sensory cues—touch, sight, smell—continually influence our relationships with one another. Using the toolbox metaphor, these are all specific tools or instruments that can foster a connection—by helping to build trust between people, stimulating physical attraction, and instilling confidence or self-assurance in a person.

Greg Sancier, the officer negotiating with the hostage taker, however, needed something more powerful and immediate—and something that would work from a distance—in his effort to establish a bond with Ed Jones.

We're going to look at how people in a variety of situations try to create a click with another person—from Greg Sancier negotiating with a hostage taker, to actors vying for a dramatic role on a national TV show, to a chef trying to create the perfect dining experience, to couples meeting online. What we've discovered is that there are five click accelerators—"ingredients" or factors involved in a click—that show up time after time across different contexts.

What are these five accelerators? Vulnerability, proximity, resonance, similarity, and a safe place. In the course of *Click* we'll examine each of these accelerators, investigating the unique roles that they play in helping us form quick-set intimacy.

The first accelerator, *vulnerability*, is perhaps the most counterintuitive of the five. Most of us think that when we make ourselves vulnerable we are putting ourselves in a susceptible, exposed, or subservient position. By revealing their inner fears and weaknesses, many feel they allow others to gain power or influence over them. But in terms of creating an instant connection, vulnerability and self-disclosure are, in fact, strengths. They accelerate our ability to connect with those around us.

Allowing yourself to be vulnerable helps the other person to trust you, precisely *because* you are putting yourself at emotional, psychological, or physical risk. Other people tend to react by being more open and vulnerable themselves. The fact that both of you are letting down your guard helps to lay the groundwork for a faster, closer personal connection. When you both make yourselves vulnerable from the outset and are candid in revealing who you are and how you think and feel, you create an environment that fosters the kind of openness that can lead to an instant connection—a click.

Back in San Jose, as Greg Sancier arrived on the scene and began his negotiation, his prediction of a long, tense night ahead proved all too true. But listen to how Sancier attempted to connect with Ed Jones. Remember, Jones was a three-striker gang member who had nothing to lose. Sancier talked to Jones for about fifteen hours that evening, on and off. "It takes time to develop that trust and good faith. The guy might say, 'Screw you! I'm going to kill everybody in here. If you're going to come in here and get me, I know you're going to kill me. Go screw yourself.' Only they use harsher language. And that goes on for hours."

But Sancier doesn't allow this animosity to get into his head or interfere with his strategy. He knows that his work is a delicate dance that can take an extended period of time. Instead of retaliating or coming across aggressively, he tried to connect with Jones. "Once I went through a tough situation myself," Sancier said, opening up. "Not like yours—but I remember, like when my mother died.' "

Jones couldn't help responding: "Your mother died?"

At that moment Sancier knew he'd made a breakthrough. "So—bam—now we're connected on that human level," he recalled. That interaction, and the emotional door it opened, transformed the whole tenor of the negotiation.

Over the course of the evening, Jones slowly began to trust Sancier; knowing he was surrounded, he came to see that his situation was hopeless. "Ultimately, he wanted to say good-bye to his mother and father." Sancier was taking a break and getting a bite to eat when all of a sudden he heard shouts of "He's coming out!" Sancier's long evening talking with Jones had paid off. "I ran out there—and a lot of SWAT guys are mad at me to this day for what happened—but I let him approach me and he actually gave me a hug." It was an unexpected ending to an intense, volatile situation. And it all came about because Sancier was willing to make himself vulnerable to Jones and build a genuine relationship with him over those long, tension-filled hours. Being willing to disclose to others the kind of person you are, to drop your protective armor, can alter the entire dynamic of a relationship.

Every Friday afternoon at the Stanford Business School, MBA candidates gather on the steps of the school for a corporate-sponsored schmooze-a-thon. The drinks are free, and the students cluster in small groups, sipping beer from red plastic cups and discussing what's on their minds—an upcoming midterm, job interviews, plans for a round of golf with alumni. Inevitably, amid the hubbub, one overhears whispering about something called "Touchy-Feely groups."

When a curious first-year student interrupts to ask what these groups are about, he or she is told, "I can't talk about it," or "It's a secret," or "It's just different from anything else."

The Stanford Business School is famous for its courses on finance, economics, operations, and statistics. But the most popular class in the entire MBA program is Interpersonal Dynamics. No one, however, mentions the course by that official course-catalog title. Even the instructors and the other faculty refer to it by its much more common nickname, "Touchy-Feely." Back when Ori himself was a first-year MBA at Stanford, he had the impression that the Touchy-Feely groups met in a secret chamber in the basement of the business school and that only the initiated were allowed to attend.

A typical course at the Stanford Business School is held in a mini-auditorium, and the environment is as intense as it is rigorous. On the first day, professors often dive right into the middle of the textbook. (Who knew the admissions people were serious when they talked about summer reading?) Students are expected to come to each class session having read several lengthy case studies. Several minutes into a class, some professors hold a raffle reminiscent of the Vietnam draft, where they pick out names of students to grill about the nuances of the material in what is affectionately known as the Socratic method. It is a business boot camp of sorts, designed to educate and toughen up students, to prepare them for the kind of rapid-fire decisions they will later face in the business world.

After a first year filled with these kinds of classes in the core curriculum, Ori was due to enter the world of Touchy-Feely. Rather than meeting in a spacious auditorium, the Touchy-Feely group convened in a fifteen-by-fifteen-foot study room. The tables in the room were all pushed up against the walls; Ori found thirteen chairs arranged in a circle. A man in his early forties entered and introduced himself: "I'm going to be your facilitator." He sat down in one of the chairs, and the rest of the students hesitantly joined him.

The members of the group looked warily at one another, waiting for the facilitator to begin, but the facilitator purposely kept silent. Lacking an agenda or even a discussion topic, various students took a stab at conversation. An hour into the session, the group was still groping desperately for something, *anything*, to talk about. To describe that first session as awkward would be an understatement.

Eventually the facilitator revealed what had previously been such a mystery about Touchy-Feely. The norms (he never talked about "rules") of these groups were fairly straightforward: the point was to talk about your emotions to the group, concentrating on how you were feeling in the "here and now." As one might expect with a high-powered bunch of students who'd spent their careers in the work world as buttoned-down consultants and fledgling investment bankers, this was much easier said than done.

Over the next couple of weeks, the members of the group took turns attempting to express their emotions to the others in the group. Because of the sensitive nature of their discussions, they agreed to maintain strict confidentiality. Soon Ori was one of those students on the steps of the school, huddled in urgent, secret conversation.

The real breakthrough in the group took place in the fourth week. "I feel weird even talking about it," one of the men in the group began. And he proceeded to share a story from his childhood that he had never told anyone up to that point. What's important is that on a scale of 1 to 10 in terms of emotional intimacy (with 1 being "Hi, how are you?" and 10 being "I'm about to reveal one of my deepest secrets"), this was close to a 10. The guy opened up in a way that no one else had up to that point in the class. What happened in this Touchy-Feely group is what happens in all of them: participants begin to share stories of their feelings—feelings over losing a fiancé, struggling with an eating disorder, even battling cancer. In other words, members of the group open up to one another and make themselves vulnerable, willingly knocking down the walls they've erected socially over the years to protect themselves from fear, pain, and potential humiliation.

What is surprising to them is that their willingness to expose themselves emotionally leads other members of the group to trust them more. As Ori told the student who shared his childhood story, "You know, I feel really close to you right now." All the students in the group felt more connected. There was an intensity to their interactions. That first student's story gave the others in the group permission to reveal their own personal fears and concerns, hidden ambitions and secret anxieties. They became more intimate, more open, more comfortable in their own skin with one another. They *clicked*. Most important, Ori observed in the Touchy-Feely classroom the same intensity and sense of engagement described by the participants in Rom's study about peak magical experiences.

To understand exactly what goes on in the Stanford

groups, it is useful to look at vulnerability through the lens of our daily language and interactions. If you were to carry around a voice recorder for the day—while you're talking to your spouse, sitting in a conference call, buying a pack of gum—and later analyze these conversations, you'd find that you could categorize them all on a scale of 1 to 5 in terms of the degree of vulnerability expressed in these interactions.

At one end of the vulnerability spectrum are what are known as *phatic* statements, statements that are not emotionally revealing. These are social niceties, such as "How are you?" and "It's nice to see you." They are more or less the motor oil or ball bearings of casual interactions. We say these things not because we want to elicit a response but rather because they smooth out any friction in our social interactions.

One step deeper, we get to the second level of vulnerability in conversation, which is referred to as *factual*. In this type of discourse, people share and seek basic bits of objective, factual data: "I live in New York." "What do you do for a living?" These are straightforward observations to which no strong opinions are attached.

Next on the scale are *evaluative* statements, which reveal our views about people or situations: "That movie was really funny." "I like your new haircut." In making such statements, we take a certain risk, because we are taking a position that is potentially in discord with others. Nonetheless, the risk is usually pretty limited.

These three levels of interactions—phatic, factual, and evaluative—constitute what we call the transactional category: communication that conveys thought-oriented (as opposed to emotional) information. It's only when we cross the threshold to the second category, connective interactions, that we really make ourselves vulnerable to other people.

The fourth level of interaction, what psychologists call *gut-level* statements, reveal our feeling-based perspective: "I'm sad that you're not here." "I'm so glad that I have you in my life." Each of these comments reveals something personal and emotionally laden about the speaker. We usually limit these types of conversations to the people who are closest to us, people whom we already trust.

Even with those we are closest to, though, we rarely venture into the fifth and most emotionally vulnerable level, what are called *peak* statements, where we share our innermost feelings, feelings that are deeply revealing and carry the most risk in terms of how the other person might respond. Here is an example: "When you said you felt I wasn't good with children, I was dumbfounded—and hurt. Do you really think I'm that insensitive? That I wouldn't make a good father? I guess at heart I'm terrified that I'm going to lose you."

What happens in Touchy-Feely is that overall communication between members of the group goes from the transactional sphere to the connective. And the result is magic. *We can help to create magical connections simply by elevating the language we use from the phatic to the peak level.*

Let's revisit Sancier in that pressure-filled hostage nego-tiation with Ed Jones. In a very real way, Greg Sancier prac-tices a form of Touchy-Feely in his hostage negotiations.

Placed in Sancier's shoes, facing an armed suspect like Ed Jones, most of us would tend to fall back on assert-ing our power. We might point out to Jones that he's out-gunned and making a terrible mistake. But Sancier goes directly against this instinct. "I always try to add that el-ement of humanness," he says. He tries to make his ap-proach highly personal.

Sancier knows he can gain more by expressing open-ness and vulnerability to the other person. "It's a very delicate situation. The suspect's trust in people—perhaps stemming from those he was supposed to trust when he was very little—is damaged. So why should he trust me?"

At its core, the challenge Sancier faces is one we all encounter. It's one thing to talk about impersonal things, such as the weather, with someone we've just met. But achieving an emotionally engaged connection is entirely different. If we make a connection that is overly vulnerable or open without proper context, our revelation can seem to come from left field and scare people away, creating dis-tance rather than a connection.

It's a problem that social psychologist Art Aron is well aware of. Aron, a professor at Stony Brook University, has spent his career studying personal relationships and inter-personal closeness. He theorizes that the key to generating intimacy with others is to gradually increase people's willingness to disclose emotionally sensitive information about themselves. While the phatic and factual levels rarely create a close personal bond, it is often important to start with them as a takeoff point for more emotionally revealing interaction.

To test the theory, Aron's research team traveled to a large university lecture hall and paired off individual students who didn't know each other. They asked each pair to go off on their own and ask each other a series of questions over the course of forty-five minutes. Half the pairs were given questions that focused on the factual and evaluative levels. These questions covered such topics as the best gift they'd ever received, what they'd done on Halloween, their favorite holiday, whether they got up early or slept in, the best TV show they'd seen in the last month, and the foreign countries they'd most like to visit. Remember, in most kinds of social gatherings, these would make for perfectly safe and appropriate conversational topics.

The other half of the pairs were also given questions that started on the factual/evaluative level—whether before making a phone call they ever rehearsed what they were going to say, or when was the last time they had sung to themselves or to someone else. But the questions slowly progressed to elicit much more revealing information:

"What are your most treasured memories?" "What roles do love and affection play in your life?" "How close and warm is your family?"

After half an hour, the questions became even more intense. The researchers asked the participants to share an embarrassing moment from their lives: the last time they cried in front of another person. Finally, they asked, "Of all the people in your family, whose death would you find most disturbing?"

You can feel, just by reading these questions, how personally revealing the conversations might become. And sure enough, the pairs in the two groups had very different reactions to the exercise. At the end of the forty-five-minute dialogues, Aron asked the students to rate how close they felt to their partner. It shouldn't be a big surprise that the second group—the ones who had reached peak-level communication—had formed a much closer bond than their small-talk counterparts.

The big surprise came weeks later, when Aron and his colleagues returned to the lecture hall to collect follow-up data. They found that many of the participants who had been assigned to the peak-communication group continued to sit together in class and reported spending time together even outside of school. The connection each of these pairs made persisted well beyond the experiment itself, just as in the Stanford Touchy-Feely course. The connection remained strong enough that it didn't die out over time.

The results are certainly intriguing. But one could argue

that they're to be expected. After all, the students were relative strangers, and it makes sense that those who had deeper conversations were more likely to keep in touch and even build on those initial friendships. The most striking part of the experiment comes when we look at how significantly and how quickly vulnerability affects a new relationship.

For the last part of the experiment, Aron's team surveyed a broad selection of students not involved with the dialogues. They asked them to think of the person they felt closest to in their lives—be it their significant other, their parent, or their best friend—and to rate how close they felt to him or her. Aron then compared these scores with the earlier participants' ratings of how close they felt to their dialogue partner. What he found was striking. The intensity of the dialogue partners' bond at the end of the forty-five-minute vulnerability interaction was rated as closer than the closest relationship in the lives of 30 percent of similar students. In other words, the instant connections were more powerful than many long-term, even lifelong relationships.

We so rarely find ourselves in situations where both individuals exhibit authentic vulnerability. But one's ability and willingness to be vulnerable can accelerate a meaningful connection. For one such pair, the connection forged in the study was so powerful that just a few months after the study, they got engaged and were subsequently married.

This same combination of self-disclosure and gradual escalation is the secret to Sancier's remarkable outcome with Ed Jones. One of the first things Sancier does when he arrives at a scene is to identify a gateway through which he can move the relationship from the transactional realm to the connective. He waits for a moment when "the suspect really wants me to understand something about himself. I could either remain intellectual about it—'Yes, it is a tough place you got yourself into'—or I could use the opportunity to dive right into it." And that's when Sancier shifts gears. "I may share with him a difficult situation I had to endure myself, in my own life." Sharing a story of a loss—for instance, the death of his own mother—builds the bridge.

When we allow ourselves to be vulnerable in engaging with another person, the emotional intensity of the conversation escalates as the other person responds in kind. He or she recognizes our willingness to be open as an invitation to take the relationship to a deeper level. Of course, the other person may back away—that is the risk we take in being open. But when someone responds in kind, then we both are acknowledging that we would like to take the relationship to a deeper level.

Researcher Susan Singer Hendrick surveyed married couples and found that self-disclosure was associated with increased levels of marital satisfaction. When Hendrick analyzed the data, she found that both self-disclosing and being the recipient of such disclosure contributed to an increase in relationship satisfaction.

A pair of Canadian psychologists named E. Sandra

Byers and Stephanie Demmons were curious about the effect of intimate sexual self-disclosure. They asked dating couples how much of their intimate fantasies, desires, and needs they shared with their partner. The researchers found that sexual self-disclosure increased both sexual and relationship satisfaction. But there's good news for the more prudish among us: general self-disclosure was just as powerful as its more intimate counterpart in boosting sexual and relationship satisfaction.

In terms of clicking with someone new, Rutgers communications professor Jennifer Gibbs and her colleagues from Michigan State University and Georgetown found that Match.com members who made an active choice to share more personal information about themselves in their profiles and in communication with others were more likely to experience success in the dating process.

Our natural desire to reciprocate by being vulnerable—and consequently take the relationship to a deeper level—is so ingrained in us that scientists have found it can even be triggered by a desktop computer. Harvard Business School professor Youngme Moon asked students to interact with a computer program she developed, which asked them to answer very personal questions about their biggest disappointments in life, the personality characteristics they were most proud of, and situations in the past that had hurt their feelings. Most of these students were reluctant to pour out their hearts and kept their responses fairly safe and guarded. For instance, when asked, "What have you done in your life that you feel most guilty about?" the over-whelming majority either lied ("Gosh, I don't think I feel guilty about anything") or skirted the question altogether ("I don't know" or "I'd rather not tell anyone"). And that's not surprising. Think how you'd react, sitting in a labora-tory, being prodded by a computer program about your in-nermost feelings.

But then Moon reprogrammed the software so that the computers raised the same questions but framed them in a self-disclosing context. She recruited a new group, also composed entirely of Harvard students, but this time around, instead of coldly fishing for responses, the com-puter seemed to make itself vulnerable, "self-disclosing" information about itself. Rather than simply asking, "What have you done in your life that you feel most guilty about?" the computer first divulged information about it-self: "There are times when this computer crashes for rea-sons that are not apparent to its user. It usually does this at the most inopportune time, causing great inconvenience to the user. What have you done in your life that you feel most guilty about?"

Remember, the Harvard participants were all well aware that computers don't have feelings. And to ensure that none of the participants mistakenly thought that they were conversing with a human being, Moon never used the pronoun "I." The computer always identified itself as "this computer."

Still, when the computer opened up, revealing "personal" information about itself, so did the students. Here, for instance, are the responses to the guilt question. While the first group tended to lie or skirt the question, the second group became quite candid: "I feel guilty about the fact that I have left my family. I am well on my way to being more successful than anyone else in my family, and I think part of my family resents it. I feel guilty because I don't relate to them in the same way I used to, and feel myself drifting away. I believe that family should be an important part of one's life, so I have trouble justifying my split from them sometimes." Or consider this equally frank response: "Well, since you brought it up . . . masturbation (that religion thing again). Also being cruel and uncaring to my mom." In other words, the students' answers were more intimate and more sincere. And when asked how they felt about the computer they interacted with, they were significantly more likely to describe it as likable, friendly, kind, and helpful.

This tendency to be more open and intimate with people who are more open and intimate with us is hardwired in us. And it is one of the most powerful mechanisms there is in forming a click between people. "What I try to do," Sancier says, "when I talk to people is to get very, very personal. They don't need to know about my qualifications or my philosophical perspectives. I just keep planting that seed that I care about them—that I want to develop trust and good faith with them. You never know what one word or phrase will make the difference. You never know how you're going to affect somebody."

Of course, vulnerability is most effective when it's genuine and sincere. Still, the response is so ingrained in us that we are naturally receptive to vulnerability—regardless of whether it comes from an inanimate computer at Harvard or a skilled Arkansas politician.

Back in June 1992, five months before the presidential election, then-governor Bill Clinton was polling in third place, trailing incumbent George H. W. Bush and third-party candidate Ross Perot. Marred by the Gennifer Flowers scandal and branded a draft dodger, Clinton's prospects for carrying the election appeared dim. Indeed, on June 3, 1992, Tim Russert placed the proverbial nail in the Clinton campaign coffin: "Clinton has fundamental problems," he declared. "The American people have made up their mind about him. He's become almost irrelevant."

It was a dire observation that didn't escape Clinton's aides and strategists. "Those of us inside the Clinton campaign," remembers George Stephanopoulos, "realized voters weren't connecting with our candidate."

As a last-ditch effort, Clinton embarked on the talk-show circuit, opening up about his personal life: his childhood, being raised by a single parent, and having an alcoholic stepfather. In other words, Clinton became vulnerable.

Now, of course, we may wonder how much of Clinton's vulnerability was strategic and how much of it was genuine. The campaign had a name for the vulnerability strategy—it was called the "Manhattan Project." So it's safe to assume that while Clinton's opening up had sincere elements, it was also very strategic. But what's important for our purposes is that Clinton's vulnerability—whatever prompted it—enabled him to form a connection with the voters in a way that no presidential candidate before him had ever done.

At the time, the decision to become vulnerable and hit the talk-show circuit was unthinkable for a presidential candidate. A presidential nominee was expected to come off as confident and strong, not as someone still affected by painful memories from childhood. Clinton was the first presidential candidate to take the truly vulnerable route. The Bush campaign was quick to label him "weird" and "wacky." But Clinton continued the vulnerability tack. Appearing on an MTV special, he took time to answer questions about how it felt "growing up in an alcoholic family and having a brother who's a drug addict." Instead of being embarrassed or shying away from these candid inquiries, Clinton embraced them. He delved into his trials and tribulations, shared the obstacles he had faced, and discussed the benefits he had gained from doing so. By the end of the month he had clocked two appearances each on the *Today* show and *Larry King Live*, in addition to interviews with *Good Morning America* and *CBS This Morning*.

At the beginning of June 1992, Clinton was polling at a favorability rating of 33 percent. By the end of the month—after he had exposed his softer side—the number had jumped to 77 percent. "I think we virtually lost the election," Bush spokesman Marlin Fitzwater would later tell Larry King, "before anybody realized the wisdom of doing these shows." But it wasn't just the face time that counted; it was how Clinton presented himself. He had succeeded in moving the discourse from the transactional sphere to the connective realm. Doing so likely helped him win the presidency.

Given the transformative effects of making ourselves vulnerable, why do we usually shy away from doing so when the opportunity presents itself? The fear is twofold: that people will take advantage of the information we give them, or that the sharing will make them feel uncomfortable or perceive us as needy. But most of all, we fail to self-disclose because we don't realize just how powerful it is in establishing instant intimacy. We are conditioned to reveal information only on a need-to-know basis. But if self-disclosure is done at the right time, with the right person, it can transform a relationship, letting the other person know that we trust them and that we want to get to know them on a deeper, more meaningful level.

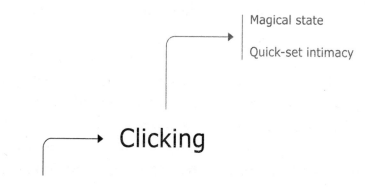

Magical state

Quick-set intimacy

Clicking

Click Accelerators

Vulnerability

Transactional
Phatic
Factual
Evaluative

Connective
Gut-level
Peak

CHAPTER 3

The Power of Proximity

There's a phrase our Jewish grandmother used to utter when a certain kind of person crossed her path: *lo yutzlach*. It translates, essentially, to "He'll never succeed." Although she knew as much about sports as a Southern Baptist is likely to know about the Yiddish language, our grandma's term neatly captured the University of Florida men's basketball team—until recently.

Year after year, the Florida Gators put together a team that they hoped would capture a national title, or at least win an invitation to the NCAA tournament at the end of each season. (Sixty-four teams from across the nation are invited to participate in the single-elimination tournament, which begins in early March.* After the first round, the thirty-two losing teams are eliminated and the winners go on to the second round. In subsequent rounds, the field is whittled down to the Sweet Sixteen, Elite Eight, Final Four, and ultimately the two teams that play in the final game for

*Starting in 1994, the tournament expanded to sixty-five teams. The two lowest-ranked teams entering the tournament battle it out for the sixty-fourth slot.

the championship.) However, despite its committed players and a well-funded athletics program, in nearly half a century the Gators failed to qualify for the tournament even once.

In 1987, for the first time in its history, the Gators finally made it to the NCAA tournament. But although the team was beginning to show some signs of progress, it still couldn't win a championship. Here is its record from 1987 to 1995.

Year	Performance in the NCAA Tournament
1987	Eliminated in the Sweet Sixteen
1988	Eliminated in the second round
1989	Eliminated in the first round
1990	Failed to qualify for the tournament
1991	Failed to qualify for the tournament
1992	Failed to qualify for the tournament
1993	Failed to qualify for the tournament
1994	Eliminated in the Final Four
1995	Eliminated in the first round

The university tried to improve its basketball team in every possible way. After a string of coaches, the Gators hired Billy Donovan—who had played college basketball himself—in 1996. In 2000, Donovan led Florida to the finals for the first time in the team's history (they lost).

Here's the team's record during Donovan's first ten years with the team:

Year	Performance in the NCAA Tournament
1996	Failed to qualify for the tournament
1997	Failed to qualify for the tournament
1998	Failed to qualify for the tournament
1999	Eliminated in the Sweet Sixteen
2000	Lost in the finals
2001	Eliminated in the second round
2002	Eliminated in the first round
2003	Eliminated in the second round
2004	Eliminated in the first round
2005	Eliminated in the second round

You get the idea. After its pinnacle 2000 tournament performance, despite the hopes of fans and subsequent seasons that began on a promising note, the Gators still weren't able to bring home a national victory.

The 2005–6 season looked like it would be one of the most challenging yet. It was Donovan's tenth year as head coach. All the stars from the previous season had graduated or turned pro, leaving behind a young, inexperienced team. With much of the previous year's starting lineup gone, the Florida basketball team entered the season unranked. The fans were bracing themselves for yet another disappointing ride.

Billy Donovan and his coaching staff realized this would be a rebuilding year and decided to give the younger players more time on the court so that they would be competitive the next year. But what happened defied everyone's expectations. After decades of trying everything imaginable, the team benefited from something surprising—a random decision by the student housing authority.

Four young sophomore players—Corey Brewer, Taurean Green, Al Horford, and Joakim Noah—had all been assigned by the housing office the previous year to live together in the Springs Residential Complex, where they shared two rooms and a bathroom. Green and Horford were the sons of NBA players; Green, a six-foot-tall point guard, was energetic and talkative, while six-foot-ten center Horford was disciplined and mature. Joakim Noah, a New Yorker, at six-eleven, playing forward, was the intellectual of the bunch. He spoke French, was interested in politics, and was always full of energy. Corey Brewer, six-foot-nine, from Tennessee, played forward as well. A student from a modest upbringing, he was a man of few words.

As Brewer would later tell the *New York Times*, the four roommates "clicked immediately." They called themselves the "oh-fours," to mark the year, 2004, when they started at the university.

The oh-fours spent as much time playing together as possible, even after practice. They'd head out to the gym or the park and challenge anyone—no matter who they were or how skilled at basketball they were—to a pickup game. The only rule the oh-fours had was that they had to play together on the same team.

Despite their enthusiasm, they didn't receive much playing time their freshman year. They spent the majority of the 2004–5 season watching the games from the bench. It was only in their sophomore year, when the varsity players left for the NBA and the coaches were left with no other choice, that the four really got a chance to play.

In Florida's first game of the 2005–6 season—facing St. Peter's College, another unranked team—the oh-fours were impressive. On the court they communicated well, played unselfishly, and were uncannily attuned to one another's strengths and abilities. As a result, the Florida team easily beat St. Peter's, 80–51.

The next day, the Gators faced Albany College. Again they won a decisive victory, 83–64. But although the team had played exceptionally well so far, the Gators had been favored to win both games.

A bigger test came the following week, when Florida was the underdog, facing two of the best teams in the league. The Gators kept their winning streak alive against Wake Forest, ranked eighteenth in the nation, pulling off a 77–72 upset. And the next day they beat sixteenth-ranked Syracuse, winning 75–70. It was the beginning of an unprecedented streak.

In fact, Florida went on to win seventeen consecutive games, with the oh-fours continually shining on the court. "I could say," head coach Billy Donovan told reporters, "I really went out and did a great job and pieced this thing together. That would be a lie."

At the end of an impressive regular season, the Gators had achieved what nobody had expected: they had won the Southeastern Conference title and secured a berth at the NCAA tournament. During "March Madness," the Gators breezed through the early elimination rounds of the NCAA tournament and made it all the way to the championship game against UCLA—a school with eleven championship titles under its belt, the most in NCAA history. The game would pit the *lo yutzlachs* against the most successful college basketball team in history. But the oh-fours did not buckle or bend—they were a force to be reckoned with. The Gators won handily, 73–57, earning Florida its first NCAA basketball championship.

It was as if the season had been scripted for a Hollywood movie. The oh-fours had brought about a Cinderella turn-around. Each of the oh-fours knew he could land a lucrative NBA contract if he wished—even as a sophomore. It was a chance to live out every basketball player's dream. Normally, such a decision is a no-brainer. When NBA teams are interested in you, you say yes. You jump at the opportunity to make the big bucks. After all, if you stay another year in college, you risk getting injured or having a disappointing season, jeopardizing a big NBA payday.

But for the oh-fours it wasn't such a clear-cut decision. The four players had become incredibly close. They loved playing together—there was a magic between them. It wasn't so easy to walk away. And so, after some soul-searching and numerous long conversations together, the oh-fours decided to stay with the Gator team.

Their performance the next season was just as spectacular: the Florida Gator team that had underperformed for decades found itself in the NCAA basketball championship game for a second year in a row, this time facing the Ohio State Buckeyes. At the half, the Gators led by nine points. They were able to hold on and win by that margin, 84–75. Florida had captured back-to-back NCAA championships.

The NBA came calling again that summer, and this time the oh-fours decided to take the plunge. Noah was drafted by the Chicago Bulls. Horford went to the Atlanta Hawks. Corey Brewer ended up in Minnesota, with the Timberwolves. And Taurean Green was grabbed by the Portland Trail Blazers.

What was the aftermath of the oh-fours' departure, you might ask? First, unsurprisingly, without the oh-fours, the Florida Gators fell back into their familiar pattern: they failed to qualify for the NCAA tournament the next two years, 2008 and 2009. Second, none of the individual oh-four players has achieved the same level of excellence in the NBA that they had playing together in Florida. Joakim Noah had disciplinary issues with the Bulls. Corey Brewer hasn't been a strong contributing force with Minnesota.

Horford played well for Atlanta but hasn't become the kind of star he was at Florida. And Taurean Green was traded from team to team before ending up playing for Greece in the European league.

Talented as they were as a group, individually the oh-fours simply weren't of superstar caliber. That fact underscores just what an astonishing feat they pulled off with the Gators. They were such a potent force on the court not because they were superior athletes but because they communicated and worked together so well as a team. The bonds the players had formed together as roommates—the connection they had made—was so powerful that it took them all the way to the NCAA championship.

In exploring the ways in which these four players clicked, we can see the impact of the second click accelerator: *proximity*. But before we return to Florida, let's travel to a police academy in Maryland, where forty-five men are about to graduate.

A few weeks after completing their requirements at the police academy, the newly minted police officers received a letter from Mady Wechsler Segal, a young professor of sociology at Eastern Michigan University. Segal was conducting a study about interpersonal attraction. She wanted to know what factors had contributed to new acquaintances hitting it off. The young professor collected detailed background information, asking each cadet which classmates in the academy he or she was most connected with. When she received the surveys back, Segal examined the data and tried to make sense of why any two cadets were more or less likely to form a connection.

From the biographical data Segal accumulated, she discovered that the factors one would expect to matter— religious affiliation, age, marital status, ethnic background, hobbies, and group memberships—had little, if any, predictive value in whether or not two cadets clicked. A bachelor who liked to watch football, for example, was just as likely to form a friendship with a family man who attended church every Sunday as he was with a fellow sports fan who was similarly single.

But there was one factor Segal discovered that had a huge effect on whether or not two cadets connected. It turned out that although how the cadets spent their free time was more or less irrelevant, their *names* were not. If you were to tell Segal a cadet's last name, in fact, she could predict with surprising accuracy which other cadets he'd become friends with.

Here was the secret behind her predictive abilities. When Segal collected her surveys, she noticed that officers who clicked together also shared one important attribute: the first letter of their last name. Officer Thomson was likely to click with Officer Taylor, Officer Adams with Officer Aaronson. The reason was simple. Just as in elementary school, the cadets were assigned seats in alphabetical order. Thompson was seated near, if not next to, Taylor—but across the room from Adams.

When the cadets listed the people with whom they had formed a close relationship, 90 percent named the individual they sat right next to. Sit even a couple of chairs farther apart and your chances of forming a close relationship with the other person were dramatically diminished. These connections weren't all of the knock-your-socks-off, instant-best-friend variety. Still, the pattern was so strong and robust that it points to an important phenomenon.

Think of all the cadets in the classroom, all the common experiences and shared interests, all the obvious reasons they might form friendships. Yet nine out of ten cadets formed a relationship with the person who sat right next to them. In other words, the single most important factor in determining whether or not you connect with another person is neither personality nor mutual interests—it is simple proximity.

Let's take a step back here. It makes sense that we're more likely to become friends with someone who lives in or grew up in the same city that we did, as opposed to someone who lives on the other side of the country. Similarly, it makes sense that we're more prone to connect with someone from the same neighborhood or, even more, from the same block. But what's interesting is the impact that proximity has in those last few feet separating two people. We usually don't give much thought to where we sit in class or in an office meeting. But in fact a couple of feet of space make a world of difference. The likelihood of clicking, of forming a meaningful connection, with someone increases exponentially the closer we are to that person. We call this phenomenon *exponential attraction*.

Which brings us back to the second click accelerator, proximity. Those last few feet really matter. Let's take a look at what a difference those few feet make in the case of apartments inhabited by a group of students living in a dorm at MIT.

The MIT apartments, hastily constructed in the years immediately following World War II, were not exactly the Ritz. There weren't enough laundry facilities, the heating was too weak to fend off the Massachusetts winters, and wherever you looked, you'd see an accumulation of dust from local factories. The factories, in turn, combined with a congested highway and the Charles River to serve as a physical buffer, isolating the units from the rest of campus life. Despite these conditions, the students in the dorm formed a close-knit community—the intricate dynamics of which illuminate the rule of exponential attraction and the success of the oh-fours, as well as the friendships developed in the Maryland police academy.

By conducting in-depth interviews with nearly every dorm resident, psychologist Leon Festinger and his colleagues were able to precisely map all the interpersonal connections between the residents. In a college dorm, or for that matter any community of people living together, you expect some individuals to be more likable and popular than others. But when Festinger and his team looked at the relationship connection map, they noticed something that couldn't be explained by random chance.

In building after building, the people living at the ends of the hall were relative outcasts compared with the rest of the dorm residents. On the other hand, students living in the center of the housing complex were likely to be the most popular kids, each with an unusually high number of connections. The center-unit inhabitants displayed no difference in personality traits, physical attributes, or behavioral patterns from their less popular counterparts. But everyone in the complex seemed to be drawn to them. And herein lies the mystery: why were the people who lived in the center of the building so much more prone to click with others than their counterparts living at the end of the hall?

One possible explanation involves selection. Those who preferred to keep to themselves or who disliked the most crowded hallways in the center of the building might select an apartment on the fringes for the peace and quiet and relative seclusion those units offered from the rest of the dorm. Similarly, the students who wanted to be in the middle of things might opt for an apartment in the center of a floor.

But there's a problem with this hypothesis. Just as the dorms themselves were not the Ritz, neither was the customer service. Students weren't able to make room requests—not for a room with a view and not for one at the end of the hall. Like the University of Florida with its basketball players, MIT randomly assigned each student to a unit.

So there had to be another explanation. Festinger's findings closely mirrored Segal's research at the Maryland police academy. When Festinger asked residents of the apartments whom they'd clicked with, a surprisingly high number—40 percent—named their next-door neighbors (living a scant nineteen feet away). But given that room assignments were completely random, it's highly unlikely—certainly not close to a 40 percent chance—that the person a resident was destined to click with just happened to be assigned to the apartment next door.

What would happen if you were to ask the same resident how she felt about the person living just two doors—or thirty-eight feet—away? She'd now be *half* as likely to have formed a close relationship. Walk yet another nineteen feet to a person living three doors down the hall and the likelihood of a close relationship would drop by half again.

What's really mind-boggling here is that simple proximity was far more critical to forming a connection or relationship than any other factor. So why *were* the students living at the ends of the halls likely to be less popular and have fewer relationships than students who lived in the center of the floor? They simply had fewer neighbors surrounding them. As a result, they were destined to make fewer connections. Inevitably, their social lives took a hit. In other words, a key factor in the college experience was determined by the random assignments of the housing office and by the rule of exponential attraction.

If proximity has such a potent effect, we'd expect to

see the same phenomenon occur beyond the confines of a student dorm—in workplaces and companies, for example, where technology is continually enabling people to work and live physically apart from one another. With technology such as e-mail, video chat, or even a simple phone, companies have been able to bring together workers from far-flung locations, and they seem to do just fine with telecommuting and virtual meetings. If our proximity theory is correct, we should see an adverse effect—a big one—on one's ability to form close connections with such colleagues.

A study conducted by Bell Communications Research examined a group of five hundred research scientists, the majority of whom held advanced degrees in engineering or computer science. These scientists all worked for the same company and were encouraged to collaborate on projects and to publish the results of their cutting-edge research. From an outside perspective, it looked as though the disadvantage of geographical distance was offset by the use of telecommunications. E-mails flew between work teams, and frequent phone conversations and conference calls allowed everyone to keep in touch. Although the scientists worked in buildings forty miles apart, as a group they made significant scientific progress and published numerous articles.

But the pattern of exponential attraction emerges when we look at the research papers published by the scientists. As the Bell research discovered, if we were to visit one of the scientists sitting at his or her desk and then walk down the corridor, there'd be a 10.3 percent chance that we'd bump into someone that scientist has collaborated with. But continue down the corridor and out to the main part of the floor, and the chances of the scientist collaborating with someone there suddenly fall by a factor of five, to 1.9 percent. And if we were to get on the elevator and visit another floor of the same building, the odds of our scientist collaborating would drop to a fraction of a percent. In other words, the odds of a scientist collaborating with someone on a different floor were about as high as his odds of collaborating with someone in a building forty miles away. The proximity rule that dictated friendships among police cadets and MIT dorm residents played an equally strong role here among the scientists. This effect is so powerful, in fact, that the odds of a scientist collaborating with someone on the same corridor were twenty-five times greater than his or her odds of collaborating with someone on a different floor.

In taking a look at these data, we have to take into account the fact that, unlike dorm assignments, office assignments in companies aren't entirely random. Physical proximity is often dictated by work departments. That is, we often sit near the people from our own department. And we're obviously much more prone to collaborate with these individuals, because they're part of the same business unit.

But when the researchers controlled for departmental

similarity, proximity remained a substantial force in terms of attraction. Scientists were *twice* as likely to collaborate with a departmental colleague on the same floor as with a departmental colleague on a different floor. Moreover, employees who worked in different departments but sat close to each other were six times more likely to form collaborative partnerships than they were with their counterparts in different departments who worked on different floors.

One would expect scientists to make decisions on whom to collaborate with based on research ability or knowledge or experience, not on whether someone is sitting in the adjacent office. Their academic reputations, their careers, their very livelihoods depend on their choice of collaboration partners. But the exponential attraction rule is so powerful that it overrides other factors.

One explanation for the power and ubiquity of the proximity rule is something psychologists call *spontaneous communication*. The term refers to unplanned, ordinary conversations and exchanges that occur when people interact serendipitously because they are in the same place at the same time. Think of seeing a neighbor at the park and the brief exchange you might have as you ask how he or she is doing. Or the brief conversation you might have with the person behind you in the supermarket checkout line as you wait to pay. Over time, these seemingly casual interactions with people can have long-term consequences.

We live in a time when, at least professionally, we're encouraged to streamline our workday and minimize these types of interactions. We're increasingly told to maximize our efficiency: write an e-mail instead of picking up the phone, attend a video conference instead of flying across the country. Virtualizing our relationships is more efficient, more focused—we get right to the core of business and don't waste time on extraneous content.

But actually there's tremendous power in these casual conversations and interactions. They create the social glue that enables the formation of deeper connections and relationships between people.

To see the power of this kind of exchange, let's look at the findings of Julien Mirivel and Karen Tracy, professors from the University of Colorado, who explored the dynamics of corporate meetings. In their study, the professors placed cameras to capture a series of weekly corporate meetings. In order to avoid being intrusive, they arrived well before the meetings, set up cameras, and pushed the record button. They then left the room, letting the workers interact as naturally as possible. One by one, the employees filed in, and eventually the two- to three-hour-long meetings began.

When Mirivel and Tracy watched the tapes later, they were struck not so much by the content of the meetings, which was what they had originally set out to study, but by the accidental footage captured *before* the meetings began. Take a look at two snippets excerpted from one such premeeting conversation:

Josh: Have you been sleeping much?

Joe: It's alright. Not too bad.

Heather: Did you have your baby? [Joe nods.] Yeah? Boy or girl?

Joe: Boy.

At first this interaction seems like ordinary chitchat. Heather and Josh (who's the boss) are learning that Joe isn't sleeping much because he has a newborn.

Joe describes what happened the day the baby was born, as two new workers, Amy and Carl, join the conversation. As you watch the conversation unfold, see if you can detect the moments where the spontaneous communication creates a form of intimacy:

Joe: I had to fly back Friday night.

Heather: Did you really?

Joe: I met [my wife] Andy at the hospital and he was born Saturday night.

Josh: What did she do, drive herself to the hospital?

Joe: No, she was . . . [She had a friend drive her.]

Amy: Um?

Joe: We had a plan. We had three plans planned out. [But I was on an airplane.] I turn my phone on as soon as we land, and I get a message that they're on their way to the hospital. So now I'm driving 95 miles per hour, I'm cruising here. I get there on

time, everything is fine. Then yesterday we're coming home and I got pulled over for speeding.

[Group laughter.]

Josh: "Look, officer, I have a brand-new baby."

Joe: Yeah, exactly. I said, "I'm lost . . . We're trying to
find this place to pick up this breast pump. I gotta
newborn in here. I wasn't paying attention."

[Laughter.]

Carl: "And by the way, do you have a breast pump—"

Joe: So he goes, "Well, alright, you're a new daddy, got
new responsibilities. Just watch it."

[Group laughter.]

Joe: Andy is dying in the back. Just cracking up.

Caught it? On the surface, this is a completely casual,
non-business-related interaction. Here's a guy with an an-
ecdote about rushing to the hospital to be with his wife as
she delivers their baby. Although he speeds, he encounters
no trouble. It's only when he drives her home from the hospital that he gets pulled over. We see a simple story. But
Mirivel and Tracy see a subtle social fabric being woven. It
starts with Josh, the boss, inquiring about how Joe is sleeping. Such an expression of concern might not be monu-
mental, but it simply wouldn't occur on an agenda-driven
business conference call. There wouldn't be space for it.
And as Joe continues his story, more people join, enabling
the entire group to share in the experience. "Josh's comment, 'Look, I have a brand-new baby,' and Carl's [inter-

jection], 'And by the way, do you have a breast pump,'"
Mirivel and Tracy point out, are attempts by others to
"reenact 'being' Joe." It's a chance for the group to bond
around a shared story. "They participate in a *joint telling*
of the event and display an understanding of and pleasure
in Joe's world," explain Mirivel and Tracy. "It is in 'fleeting'
conversational moments, much like this one, that relationships at work are nurtured, preserved, and managed."

Think of the Maryland police cadets. When you sit next
to someone, you're more likely to have casual conversations about the weather or yesterday's sports game. You
have an opportunity to interact and get to know the other
person. Or if you're a student at the MIT dorm, you find
yourself chatting with your neighbor about class schedules
or the upcoming midterms. Before long, almost without
noticing it, these interactions become the groundwork for
friendship.

Without such spontaneous interactions, it's harder to
form relationships with others. There is no social glue to
help bring you together. And without that social glue, conflict is more likely to arise when one person misinterprets
another's actions or behaviors.

It's easier to gain an appreciation of the impact of spontaneous communication when we see what happens when
it's missing. Professors from Stanford's Center for Work,
Technology and Organization and MIT's Sloan School of
Management closely studied the quality of relationships
among work teams of a single multinational corporation.

They interviewed forty-three teams ranging in size from three to twenty-one employees. While some of the teams were based in the same building, others worked across a broad geographical distance. As the exponential attraction theory would suggest, those teams that were physically close experienced much less task-specific conflict than the other teams. That is, they found it easier to agree on a business strategy for moving forward. The members of the teams that were physically close were also much more likely to *like* one another—and they had a dramatically lower incidence of interpersonal conflict. When the researchers talked to the team participants, they found that the daily interactions between them significantly reduced conflict of all kinds. Their casual conversations—or spontaneous communication—"was associated with a stronger shared identity and more shared context." In other words, they had developed closer personal relationships with other members of the team, which led to more cooperation and less friction.

It was that same phenomenon that changed the lives of the oh-four freshman basketball players at the University of Florida. They shared the excitement of being away from home at a new school, the novelty of sharing a room, and the difficulties of working out living situations together. They learned about each other's likes and dislikes, hopes and fears. They experienced the incredible high of playing basketball together in front of packed arenas at the college level. Now think about how different their relationships would have been had they been housed in different dorms, or if they'd had rooms on different floors or even down the hall from one another. Imagine what a difference that close proximity—the last few feet—made. After all, it was their proximity that led to endless conversations and exchanges, as well as the spontaneous decisions to go out and play pickup games, which ultimately led to the kind of powerful bond that transformed their performance on the court.

But what if we take words completely out of the equation? Yes, some encounters yield spontaneous conversation, but sometimes not a single word is exchanged. Think of the nod we might give to the woman we see waiting at the train station each morning, or the clerk at the post office. Psychologists call such interactions "passive contacts." But these contacts, too, register in our consciousness. The more passive contacts we share with another person, research has shown, the more likely we are to gravitate toward him or her.

Richard Moreland and Scott Beach, psychologists from the University of Pittsburgh, investigated this tendency over a semester in one of the university's large lecture halls. They began by selecting four women who were all the same age and had a similar physical appearance. To ensure that the women were perceived in similar ways, the researchers took pictures of the women and showed them to a randomly selected group of participants, who ranked each woman's picture on likability, attractiveness, and perceived friendliness. All the women scored about the same.

Next, the women were asked to attend a personality psychology course held in a lecture hall that sat two hundred students. None of the students knew that an experiment was under way. The researchers instructed the first of the four women to attend fifteen class sessions. The second woman was asked to attend ten sessions. The third was asked to attend only five classes. And the last woman attended none of the sessions.

Each woman arrived at the lecture hall a few minutes before class began. She was instructed to walk slowly down toward the front of the hall and sit where she could be seen by all the other students. During the lecture, she simply listened and took notes. A few minutes after the class ended, the woman would walk slowly toward the back of the hall and leave. To ensure that the women engaged in only passive contacts, the researchers instructed them to remain aloof and distant: "None of the women was allowed to interact (verbally or nonverbally) with the other students." When one of the women was approached by another student, she was told to simply turn away and ignore him or her.

The rest of the students, meanwhile, had no idea that the experiment was going on. They might see the women come and go, but without ever exchanging a word with them, how much attention would they pay to a single classmate in a lecture hall with two hundred others?

At the end of the term, the students in the class were shown pictures of each woman and asked whether they recognized her. On average, the women appeared familiar to only a tenth of the students. None of the students pointed to the pictures and claimed, "Yes, she attended the class I was in." Even the students who said they'd seen one of the women didn't know where they had seen her. In other words, the passive contacts went completely unnoticed on a conscious level.

On a subconscious level, though, it was a different story. Look at what happened when the students were asked to evaluate how interesting, attractive, unselfish, popular, unconceited, intelligent, warm, honest, successful, and sincere each woman seemed. Remember, an independent panel had scored the women equally on these criteria. But something was triggered as a result of the women being in the classroom during the semester that changed how the students in the class perceived them. Simply put, the more sessions a woman attended, the more attractive she was perceived as being. And the gulf between the woman who attended fifteen sessions and the one who attended none was enormous. Even though the overwhelming majority of students didn't remember any of the women, simply being seen more often by the students made the women more attractive to them at a subconscious level.

"We were surprised by the relatively strong effects of mere exposure on attraction," the study's authors reported. "Students liked these women better, without necessarily regarding them as more familiar." In other words, the more familiar a person is, even subconsciously, the more appealing he or she becomes.

And it doesn't end with attraction. The students in the class were next asked: "Imagine you met the woman and learned more about her. What would be the probability (0–100) that you'd become friends?" The woman who was a no-show and the woman who attended only five classes scored 41 and 43, respectively. The women who attended ten and fifteen classes, however, scored 57 and 60. Just showing up and being seen made the women appear more attractive and more friendly. The students also said they would much rather spend time with the women who were more frequent attendees. That's the power of physical proximity.

What this suggests is that people are exponentially more likely to form a relationship—to click—with people who live or work close by. Even passive contacts can be a powerful influence on whom we click with. The old adage that familiarity breeds contempt just isn't true. In fact, familiarity actually breeds regard.

Nearly every day we make decisions involving our proximity to other people. Knowing what the research reveals, it makes much more sense in a business setting to attend a meeting in person than to dial in, to walk over to a colleague's or employee's desk rather than sending an e-mail. It makes more sense to simply stand closer to someone you want to meet at a party than to look across a crowded room.

The phenomenon of clicking with another person is clearly a confluence of factors. It's about the bridges we form with others by allowing ourselves to be vulnerable with each other. And it's about the exponential effect of proximity. But as we'll see in the next chapter, it's also about those moments when we're truly present and connected with others and with everything around us.

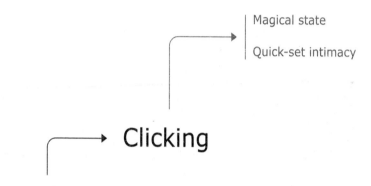

Magical state

Quick-set intimacy

Clicking

Click Accelerators

Vulnerability

Transactional
  Phatic
  Factual
  Evaluative

Connective
  Gut-level
  Peak

Proximity

Exponential Attraction
  Spontaneous communications
  Passive contacts

CHAPTER 4

When Everything Clicks

Mike Welch was preparing to take the stage in front of an audience that was, if not outright hostile, certainly less than welcoming.

By day Mike Welch is the manager of a Barnes & Noble bookstore in Los Gatos, California. But his dream, his passion, has always been stand-up comedy. "I was the class clown in school," he told us, standing near the front of his bookstore, surrounded by stacks of new arrivals. "All the way back to elementary school, I had the fantasy of being a comedian someday." When Welch moved to San Francisco he was finally able to give his dream a shot.

But as any aspiring comic knows, it's not easy being an unknown. The sobering fact is that the audience isn't really there to see *you*. They're there because they went out to a bar featuring a comedy night, and you happen to be part of the entertainment. Or they're there for another, more famous act, and you're onstage to help warm the audience up. And the moment you fall off your game, the audience is quick to tune you out.

"I would rather have someone heckle me and yell out, 'You suck,'" Welch reflected, "than face apathy." There's nothing worse than an audience who plainly just doesn't care; apathy is a killer in comedy. "There's nothing you can do. There's no energy to work with. It's like you're talking into a black hole sucking everything out of the room." Each night, Welch had to try anew to find a way to connect with his audience. "And it took me about six years to figure it out—believe it or not. Ultimately, I wrote it down on top of my set list: *connect*."

How can one establish an instant connection when the other person or group isn't interested?

On one particular night, Welch found himself in a situation where he needed desperately to connect. The evening started on an optimistic note. Welch had received an invitation to open for the Righteous Brothers. "It was the first big-name act I had opened for," he remembers. "I mean, I listened to them as a kid, my sister loved them, and all that. They put me in this big room—I felt like I was a big star."

All those years developing and fine-tuning his act, all those evenings performing in front of sparse audiences for little money, were finally paying off. Welch might not have been headlining, but he got a taste of the star treatment. "They gave me enough food for twenty people and fifty bottles of water in various shapes and sizes."

Naturally, he was nervous. Here he was, about to open

for a show-business legend. "Before I went out," Welch confided, "I thought, 'I'm going to die.' The place was packed; there must have been a couple of thousand people in that auditorium. It was a full three-camera shoot."

As he was thinking about the set ahead of him, Welch heard a knock on his dressing-room door. It was the master of ceremonies, a local radio DJ, who wanted information about how to introduce Welch. "He basically writes down my entire résumé," he remembered, "I tell him, 'I've done this, I've done that.'" But the warm introduction Welch hoped for was not to be.

"As a comedian, when you first get onstage," Welch explained, "those first few minutes are critical for you to get your footing. And here comes this MC, and what does he do? He goes out and says—word for word—'All right, everybody, I'm glad you listen to our radio station. We've got some kind of comedian, but I forget his name. Let's bring him on.'" Welch knew he had to turn the audience around, to connect with them—quickly. "I couldn't just open with my act. I would've been doomed." It was a do-or-die moment.

Up to this point in the book, we've explored how one can foster an immediate connection with other people, whether on a date or in an office situation. Now we want to look at those times when we feel a strong connection to *everything* around us, those moments in our lives when everything feels exactly right and we are completely in tune with whatever we're engaged in and with the immediate world around us—when we are in the flow, or, to use a sports catchphrase, in the zone.

It is a state that many of us are familiar with but for which we often don't have a common language. We're familiar with the phrase *being in the zone* from basketball and other sports, where it refers to when a player is on top of his or her game and just can't seem to miss. But being in the zone can occur at any moment in our lives—when we're immersed in a project or playing a piece of music. We've all experienced times in our lives when we just felt in sync with everything around us. It occurs when you are having coffee with a friend and are so into the conversation that you barely notice the time flying past. Or you are in the middle of a work project that has been dragging along, but one day you are able to focus in a heightened way and everything just seems to come together. We call this state *resonance*. It results from an overwhelming sense of connection to our environment that deepens the quality of our interactions.

Think of driving a car down the highway. Sometimes we're frustrated by the traffic around us, we're distracted by a phone call, or we fall victim to highway hypnosis. But most of us have also had experiences where the car is almost an extension of ourselves, where we're fully aware of and in tune with everything around us, when we feel completely in command or control.

To explore this phenomenon further, we wanted to get inside the head of someone who relies on that kind of shift or click, that heightened focus, for a living. "It's . . . when the race car is talking back to you," legendary driver Mario Andretti told us. In car racing, as in any other sport, one has good days and bad days. And clearly there are good drivers, and then there's Mario Andretti.

Andretti was describing to us how the car reacts on the road, when suddenly he stopped himself midsentence and his manner changed. He was remembering back to the 1978 Grand Prix of Italy at Monza and his race against rising star Gilles Villeneuve. For the majority of the race, Andretti was tailing Villeneuve, who was driving aggressively. Andretti deliberately kept himself within Villeneuve's field of vision. "I sort of tried to pass him," he recalled. "I made it look like I was trying and trying, but I had no intention of actually passing. It got to the point where Villeneuve probably felt, 'There's no way he's going to get me.' And then I even distanced myself further. I gave him a little space so that he wouldn't feel threatened."

Andretti maintained this strategy all the way to the final lap. But it was a high-risk strategy—if he couldn't overtake Villeneuve in the final lap, he'd lose the race. "I fought, fought, fought. There are not too many corners where you can attack for a pass. I figured there was one move that I could make and get away with." Andretti was down to this final opportunity, thinking, "This has got to work." On the final turn of the race, he sped up to overtake Villeneuve. "I did, and I got him. I remember every second of it, even though it was a long time ago."

Was Andretti driving well? Absolutely. Was he maneuvering a finely tuned car? Yes. But as Andretti described the race, his voice went up a notch, his energy escalated, and we could sense his excitement. It was as if he were feeling that sense of being especially alive all over again, in just thinking about the race.

Andretti's experience illustrates an important finding made by psychologist Mihaly Csikszentmihalyi, who interviewed athletes, artists, and surgeons to get a sense of those moments when they felt fully engaged and absolutely on top of their game or profession. Csikszentmihalyi described these moments when we're "on" or "in the zone" with the term *flow*. And flow, in fact, is the first of two components that make up a state of resonance.

Csikszentmihalyi wanted to identify the conditions under which flow is most likely to occur. There is something hard to capture about flow; it's not something we can summon simply by wishing it. At its essence, Csikszentmihalyi found, flow requires mastery of a task and being adequately challenged. For instance, to experience flow while playing chess, you've got to have a solid enough mastery of the game—years and years of studying and practice—and you've got to play against an opponent who can adequately challenge you.

In the case of the Grand Prix, one reason Andretti felt

so alive was because he was performing a task that he had mastered—racing a car—and he was competing against one of the best race-car drivers in the world.

Back in the concert hall, Mike Welch was far from feeling in the flow. But just as Andretti knew he had to resort to carefully considered strategy and psychological maneuvers in order to overtake Villeneuve, Welch realized he had to reframe the situation by engaging in a figurative chess match with the master of ceremonies. "I faced the crowd," he told us, "all two thousand of them, and I said, 'Let's do this introduction over again.'" The audience didn't quite know where Welch was going with all of this. "Pretend I'm the MC, okay?" Welch told them. "This is how the MC should have done it, ladies and gentlemen." Welch then proceeded to introduce himself with the gusto and exaggerated praise he thought he deserved. In so doing, all of a sudden Welch started feeling as if he was in the zone. His years in front of tough audiences had given him a mastery of his craft, and the MC had provided a worthy challenge. The two elements combined to put Welch in the flow. "It was incredible," he told us. "I was beginning to feel on top of my game; I just knew what to do next." Figuratively speaking, instead of being stuck in traffic, Welch was now acting like he was racing in the Grand Prix.

Flow, of course, isn't exclusive to the realm of competition. We may experience a state of flow, for example, when we're working on a home project or tinkering with a familiar recipe to find a new way to make the dish come together. But it always involves a challenge. For Andretti, being in the flow allowed him to be one with the car and perform to the utmost of his abilities.

For Welch, however, being in the flow wasn't enough. Challenged and on top of his game—in the flow—Welch might have been able to deliver his comedy routine fantastically well, with just the right nuances and timing. But in order for him to really succeed onstage, he also needed to connect with his audience. You can tell fantastic jokes all day long, but unless you connect with the audience, it's all for naught. After the MC's introduction, the two thousand people watching the comedian were mentally and emotionally checked out, disconnected. To overcome that, Welch needed to achieve the second component of resonance: a quality called *presence*.

Think of presence on a continuum. At one end of the spectrum, we can be completely disengaged and unaware of those around us. If we're riding a crowded subway, for example, while we might physically be present inside the train car, surrounded by other passengers, we typically don't relate to them except as objects to avoid. At the other extreme there's something we call *transformative presence*—a meaningful interaction that touches the lives of those involved in a uniquely profound manner.

Jill Anderson, a nurse at Saint Alphonsus Regional Medical Center in Boise, Idaho, studied transformative presence in her work with gravely ill cardiac patients. While medication and technology certainly play a vital part in patient health, they aren't always enough, she realized. And so Anderson set out to study the effect of presence on the patient's overall well-being. It was a one-woman experiment in making connections.

One of her encounters was with an elderly patient in the late stages of heart failure. The man arrived at Anderson's clinic barely able to breathe and suffering from exhaustion. His condition was critical. But instead of focusing only on his chart, Anderson sat down next to the hospital bed and held his hand for a few minutes. When he looked away in silence, Anderson stayed in the room. Sensing his discomfort, she asked him if he was feeling afraid. It was a simple question, really, but one very rarely asked in that setting by a medical professional. Anderson was not only monitoring the patient's physical symptoms but also being attentive to his emotional and spiritual state, taking the time to engage him on a deeper level.

All of a sudden, the patient began confiding in her. "I'm afraid that I'm dying. That is all I've been thinking about for the last six months," he confessed. "I have lived a good life, been a good husband and father, and have only one regret in my life. I mistreated someone at work many years ago. I was new to the job, and one of my first responsibilities was to fire someone. I wish I could go back and apologize to him, but it's too late to change anything. I guess I just have to forgive myself and try to let it go." The patient looked Anderson in the eyes and continued, "I've never told this to anyone before. I'm so relieved to get it off my chest."

The intensity of the moment was palpable to patient and nurse alike. It was the type of connection that never would have happened had Anderson simply checked the chart. She needed to become present so that the patient felt seen and understood—and thus was willing to expose a part of himself he had never shared before.

Because presence plays such an important role in the overall health of the patient, research in health care has uncovered four components that enable us to become present. The first of these is *intentionality*, which means entering an interaction with a sense of purpose and conscious awareness. Intentionality means giving the interaction our undivided attention, instead of going through the motions or being preoccupied with other things.

The next component of presence is *mutuality*: being open and available to meet the other person where they are. Mutuality means focusing on the shared aspects of trust and honesty involved in the relationship, rather than giving advice or trying to solve a problem.

Being present isn't just about putting our emphasis on the other person. The third component, *individuality*, refers to being authentic and aware of our own genuine emotional reactions.

Finally, presence requires *attentiveness*, demonstrating care through active involvement. Attentiveness is about actively listening, asking a person to elaborate, sharing our own reactions, and generally demonstrating to the other person that we're an active participant in the interaction. To become present, we arrive with intention, we listen and mutually interact, and we remain in touch with our individual selves and attentive to the environment and those around us.

It's what Anderson did when she engaged with the cardiac patient. And it's exactly what Welch, onstage, had to do with his audience. He needed to find a way to connect with them in the same way that Anderson had been able to connect with her patient.

"I knew that I couldn't just get up there and start my act. I had to meet them where they were," Welch recalls. And the way to do that was to get the audience on his side—even if they were just humoring him. "I had to be there with them, to train them on what to do," Welch recalls. "I said, 'Now, when I run off the stage, you're going to cheer like crazy.' And so we went through it and they just stood up and they went nuts."

Interestingly, the power of presence lasts well beyond that particular moment of interaction. Studies conducted on presence in the relationship between health care provider and patient found that when health care providers were truly engaged, patients developed a dramatically increased sense of trust and safety. Moreover, the patients actually felt better—their morale and overall sense of well-being were significantly improved—even weeks later. All from caregivers' simply being more attuned to the patient.

We've seen the same pattern in other forms of clicking—a single interaction can substantially affect the long-term characteristics of a relationship. When we achieve resonance—the combination of flow and presence—that state doesn't just temporarily alter the relationship; it actually changes those around us.

As we'll soon see, resonance doesn't just make us feel more connected to our surroundings; research shows that at its core, resonance is contagious. We tend to match the emotions of those around us. For example, we're more prone to become stressed when we're around someone who is high-strung. And we're more likely to be in a good mood when others around us are laughing. Indeed, psychologists have found that we're thirty times more likely to laugh at a joke in the presence of others than if we hear it when we're alone. In the same vein, we feel more connected with others when we're around someone who is experiencing resonance.

Since 1998, chef Lidia Bastianich has hosted a series of cooking shows on PBS—*Lidia's Italian-American Kitchen*, *Lidia's Family Table*, and *Lidia's Italy*. To viewers, there's something mesmerizing about the way she cooks. She takes her time, explaining to her audience where she got her ingredients and how she plans to use them to re-create an old family recipe. "Food is my medium," Bastianich says. "I communicate with it. It's part of my whole history.

"My family lived in a very simple setting," she told us.

"We had a garden, where my grandma grew potatoes. I picked them out of the earth—they were still warm. It's almost like they were alive. And ever since then I've had a primal connection with food." Her relationship to food, to cooking, frequently puts Bastianich in a state of flow in the kitchen.

Typically, we interact with chefs by eating their dishes at a restaurant or by buying their cookbooks and using their recipes. Rarely do we get to hear their frame of mind as they prepare a meal. And here's where presence enters the equation.

Bastianich recounted the time when she was invited to prepare a special meal for Pope Benedict XVI during a visit he made to the United States. She didn't want just to serve him a good meal; she wanted him to experience an emotional connection with the dinner, to enter that same sense of flow she often experienced. "I wanted to awaken for this pious man something deep and meaningful." She decided to prepare chicken soup, kugel, strudel—"all the things that he most likely had eaten in his childhood in Germany." Because the dinner was to take place just after his birthday, Bastianich surprised him with a cake. "We even sang to him. We even gave him a knife to cut the cake, and he didn't know what to do. So I took his hand in mine and we cut the cake and I said, 'Your Holiness, I hope you enjoyed the meal.' And he looked at me and he said, 'These are the flavors of my mother.' I lit up. I had achieved what I wanted.

He was connected back to his childhood." In essence, the pope was caught up in the resonance that Bastianich had projected.

When we're around someone who is in a state of resonance, we are more likely to enter that state as well. We are more likely to click.

Of all the people who watch her shows, Lidia Bastianich has been most surprised by the effect of the resonance she projects on autistic children. "I get letters from their parents—and I get them continuously, so it's not a one-time situation—'My child is captivated when he watches you.'" Autistic children typically have a very difficult time connecting with other people. Yet they tend to sit glued to Lidia's program. One mother wrote to Lidia, "I taped three of your shows, one after another—which means an hour and a half—and my child, who usually doesn't stay still, stood there for the entire time and watched you."

Bastianich is not completely sure what it is about her actions, tone, or approach that these autistic children gravitate toward. "Maybe it's my tonality that gives them comfort. But there is some connection that they're able to feel." At times Bastianich has invited autistic kids to come watch her cook in person. "Sometimes they can be shy," she said, and went on to tell us about one such encounter. "After the presentation, I approached the mother and then began talking to her son. And slowly he came close. And ultimately I got a hug and a kiss from him. You see the tears in his mother's eyes. It was just unbelievable."

One explanation for the response Lidia Bastianich engenders in her viewers is that she is so immersed in her craft—so resonant—that just being in that space with her, watching her create her culinary magic, brings about a similar state of magic in those who watch her.

The contagiousness of resonance can be traced neurologically to the phenomenon of mirror neurons. Italian scientists studying macaque monkeys noticed that when the animals engaged in goal-oriented behaviors (grasping, holding, tearing), neurons in their premotor cortex became very active. This region of the brain—in monkeys and humans alike—is responsible for coordinating physical movement. It stands to reason that it would become active when the monkeys were in the midst of a physical action. The interesting finding came when these same macaque monkeys were sedentary—not performing any task at all—other than observing humans engaging in goal-oriented behavior. Simply watching the humans activated the macaques' own premotor cortex. It was a literal case of monkey see, monkey do (at least as far as their brains were concerned).

These copycat neurons have been called mirror neurons because they appear to imitate others' actions, even when the subject itself is not engaged in that particular behavior. "Virtually all mirror neurons," noted neuroscientists Giacomo Rizzolatti and Laila Craighero, "show congruence between the visual actions they respond to and the motor responses they code." In other words, in the case of the macaque monkeys, it's as if the monkeys were experiencing the human action they were observing.

The same mirror neuron activity has been seen in humans. But what is imitated is not just behaviors but emotions as well. When participants observed images of other people experiencing pain, for example, the subjects' own pain region exhibited a flurry of activity. Though the participants had not been subjected to any pain whatsoever, their neurobiological mechanism acted as if they had.

There's something quite human about this tendency. More than any other animal, we tend to empathize with the feelings and qualities that we perceive in others. This empathy, this contagiousness, affects adults as well as children. It is something Fred Berner, executive producer of NBC's prime-time series *Law & Order*, considers on the job every day.

We met with Berner in front of New York City's Chelsea Piers, where he was surrounded by an entourage of actors clad in baseball caps and trendy T-shirts. The group was making its way to a casting session and was already running a few minutes late. It was a chilly afternoon; the wind had an especially strong bite that day at the piers overlooking the Hudson River. Berner, with his shaggy silver hair, wool sweater, and designer jeans, was certainly not the tallest or the loudest person in the crew, but it was clear he was the guy in charge.

Fred Berner's professional life is one walk-and-talk meeting after another. True to form, as we walked, the location scouts were peppering Berner with questions about next week's episode and some technically challenging shots at the courthouse.

If you were to observe Berner amid this fast-paced scrimmage, two things might surprise you. First, Berner doesn't fit the stereotype of a prickly producer. He cracks jokes easily about New York cabbies and a moment later asks a production assistant how his cousin is recovering from her knee operation. The second surprise is just how strong a role resonance—and, more specifically, its contagiousness—plays for Fred. "People are always surprised when I tell them that my job is all about being on the hunt for magic."

Berner explains, "Any number of producers will tell you what's the most important part of putting together a solid show. And it's not what most people think. It comes down to casting. Some guys will say, 'Casting is 98 percent of it.' Or some will say, 'Casting is 90 percent of it.' But regardless of the numbers, casting is huge. It's just huge."

Watching the show at home, viewers don't realize that the convenience store clerk who says a couple of short lines was picked from among thirty or forty actors vying for the part. Each *Law & Order* episode has approximately thirty of these speaking parts. Multiply that by the number of actors auditioning for each role each week, and you get a sense of how much of Berner's life is consumed by casting. "Over the course of a single season," Berner told us, "I see probably seven to eight thousand actors."

That is what Berner was doing down by the river that day. The entourage entered the Chelsea Piers office building through a pair of glass doors and continued down a narrow hallway that looked like the inside of a warehouse. You'd never guess it was a production facility were it not for signs on the doors with labels such as "Special Victims Unit Art Department."

Continuing up the elevator, Berner made a right and walked into the waiting area, where a dozen or so auditioning actors sat around cafeteria-style tables. What was uncanny about this scene was just how similar all the actors looked. It was as if someone had put in an order for a group of balding fifty-year-old men, a clutch of attractive twentysomething redheads, and a handful of unshaven hipsters in their thirties.

One by one these actors entered the casting room to audition for Berner and his team. The tension in the room was palpable. For the actors it's an unnerving experience. But imagine for a moment what it's like to be Fred Berner, seeing actor after actor and trying to anticipate which one is going to click with the rest of the cast and with the viewing audience. "You want to find a relationship that's going to produce a rapport among the people on the set," Berner explained. "That's what brings magic to the show. You have millions of viewers tuning in each week, and you've got to give them something that makes them sit up and watch."

At the end of the day, after seeing a string of sixty-five actors back to back, Berner went through the list of prospects with his team, nixing one after another. The problem wasn't that the actors weren't accomplished (most, in fact, were successful professionals) or that they had bombed their auditions. Nor was it really that Berner was overcritical. It was just, Berner explained, that "there's something that's difficult to put into words—a certain way an individual comes across. And when it's there, you can feel it. You know that it's right."

To illustrate this point, Berner took us back to 2007, when one of the show's most beloved stars, Sam Waterston—who played Assistant District Attorney Jack McCoy—was getting a fictional promotion to the much less visible role of district attorney. This presented a particularly difficult challenge for Berner. Waterston had become synonymous with *Law & Order*, and Berner knew that his replacement had to capture both his charisma and his likability.

"But that's easier said than done," Berner told us. He knew that the show's audience equated Waterston with the role. The replacement would have to be more than just an excellent actor. He'd have to be someone that reluctant audiences would quickly bond with.

"We had some really, really fine actors who screen-tested for the role of the assistant DA," Berner told us. "But it didn't quite gel." With each actor, Berner and his team would ask themselves whether he would resonate with the audience.

"We had all the actors read a summation to the jury,"

Berner recalls. Because it was such an important role, all the top brass were there. "I was sitting with Dick [Wolf, the show's creator], and one actor would read the lines, and another actor would follow."

The thing about such auditions is that regardless of how compelling the script is, or how talented the actor, after the fourth or fifth audition in which an actor delivers the same lines, you find yourself becoming desensitized. One audition blends into the next. An actor comes, an actor goes.

The atmosphere changed radically, though, when a candidate by the name of Linus Roache, a former member of the Royal Shakespeare Company, stepped into the room.

Now, someone with a British theater background wouldn't immediately come to mind as a natural fit for a fast-paced New York City courtroom drama. But Berner recalls, "Although Linus was reading the same lines we'd heard all afternoon, there was something different about him. As soon as he started delivering the lines, all of a sudden, everybody who was sitting in 'video village' here behind the monitors perked up. Dick looked up from his BlackBerry. There was something special, almost transcendent; you could feel it. It just clicked with Roache. And I said to myself, 'Whoa, who's that guy?' He was able to take a monologue that we had been through at that point dozens of times, and all of a sudden the thing had a truth to it."

Hearing Berner describe it, you can almost imagine sitting there with him in the casting session. Suddenly, the energy in the room shifted from evaluating actors and trying to stay awake to an electric excitement. However mentally absent the team had been before, it was now fully engaged, fully there. "It's like somebody is sitting around the campfire and you're thoroughly engrossed," Berner explained. "That's what it felt like. Particularly in a room where there's tension and people not feeling comfortable, it being five in the afternoon, when there's already no energy. All these elements that conspire to make you not present, not open. But when it's happening, you're in it. By the time Linus finished reading his part, we all looked at each other and we went, 'Holy shit. Here we go. We got ourselves an actor.'"

And that is the kind of resonance that happened to Mike Welch as he continued his act. On that night, right after the worst introduction a comedian could receive, Welch would have the single best performance of his career. After reframing the horrendous introduction he had received from the MC as a challenge—an opportunity to get into the flow—Welch looked for a way to take the second step of becoming present by making a connection with the audience, in the same way that nurse Jill Anderson was able to connect with her patient.

In his six years in the business, Welch had learned that if something unexpected happens—if a joke doesn't go right or if a heckler makes a snide comment or a waitress spills a tray of drinks, and that's where the attention and energy of the crowd is—then you can't ignore it. You have to react; you have to seek resonance. In this case, once the audience empathized with Welch over the muffed introduction, it became a common experience they had all shared.

Listening to Welch's story, we wondered how he was able to pull the metaphorical rabbit out of the hat—did he tell a great joke that had the audience rolling? But the power of resonance is subtle. Lidia Bastianich isn't one of those brash individuals whose ego demands the room's attention. Linus Roache nailed the *Law & Order* audition because he was able to simplify things and get inside the role of the assistant district attorney. That night during the show, Welch didn't come up with some new, hilarious joke out of thin air. He delivered the same material as always, but this time the MC's introduction forced Welch to become resonant with his audience. And that resonance was contagious; the audience caught the bug. "After the show," he told us with a smile, "people were coming up to me and asking for *my* autograph. That's how well it went. They told me, 'I didn't realize you'd be that funny.' "

Since then, Welch hasn't gone on to become a comedy star. He doesn't have an HBO special. He's not expecting to pack thousand-seat theaters. In fact, these days, Welch is working full time managing the Barnes & Noble store. But that night he shone.

It is resonance that lets you nail an audition or mesmerize a meeting and achieve a magical performance. It results in a kind of "click" with an entire crowd. But although it may feel as though it occurs like a bolt of lightning, in reality it is not so unpredictable. The fact is that we can, even—or especially—under pressure, induce a state of resonance and achieve a sense of flow by consciously making ourselves more present with others. And its power is contagious.

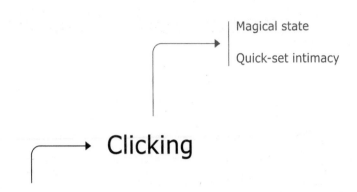

Magical state

Quick-set intimacy

Clicking

Click Accelerators

Vulnerability

Transactional
Phatic
Factual
Evaluative

Connective
Gut-level
Peak

Proximity

Exponential Attraction
Spontaneous communications
Passive contacts

Resonance

Flow

Presence
Intentionality
Mutuality
Individuality
Attentiveness

CHAPTER 5

The Seductive Power of Similarity

Twenty-year-old Kelly Hildebrandt came home from work one day in February 2008, sat at her computer, and indulged in a guilty pleasure: conducting searches for her name on the Internet. She logged in to Facebook. "It was almost midnight," she remembers. "I just wondered whether anyone else out there had my name." She wanted to see whether *her* Facebook face would come up.

It didn't. Instead of her own profile, the image that popped up was of a guy with short-cropped hair and a big welcoming smile who lived in Lubbock, Texas. Kelly Hildebrandt, meet Kelly Hildebrandt.

"He was cute," she told us. So she sent him a message telling him that she had the same name and that she just wanted to say hi.

After sending the message, Kelly checked her Facebook account each day for the next few days. "I was curious to see if he would respond. Was he a jerk or a nice guy? Three or four days later he wrote back, and he was so nice."

"I had actually done the same type of search a year and a half before that and didn't come up with anybody," remembers Kelly (the boy from Lubbock). "And then Kelly found me."

Getting a message from Kelly Hildebrandt confused Lubbock Kelly for a moment, until he realized this Kelly Hildebrandt was a girl from another state. He was intrigued. "It didn't hurt that she was cute," he admits.

It turned out to be a match made in cyberheaven. Facebook messages turned into phone calls. Before long, twenty-year-old Kelly realized that she liked her alter ego as more than just a friend.

Kelly in Lubbock got mixed reactions from his friends for falling for a girl with the same name. Some people thought it was weird. Others found the coincidence intriguing.

Two months later, the Kellys decided to meet in person. Kelly in Lubbock made the trip from Texas to Florida, where his alter ego lived. They hit it off immediately.

So the Kellys began dating. "We both go to church," explained Kelly (girl)—the two refer to themselves as "Kelly (boy)" and "Kelly (girl)." "We're very family-oriented people, and we're both pretty outdoorsy, active, and constantly doing stuff. We both like to cook. We both hate scary movies."

The story had the kind of happy ending that made for a compelling news story (especially amid the dark days of the financial meltdown). NBC filmed a segment called "A Tale of Two Kellys." The London *Daily Telegraph* ran a headline that read, "Kelly Hildebrandt to Marry Kelly Hildebrandt."

Although the story of the two Kellys is a charming, stranger-than-fiction account, it also proves the power of the fourth click accelerator we've identified: *the seductive power of similarity*.

To better explain this, we'd like to introduce you to a professor by the name of Donn Byrne, who grew up in the days well before Facebook, the Internet, or even computers. Byrne's father was a cotton broker, which meant the entire family moved frequently. Young Donn bounced from school to school growing up. "In the ninth grade I was entering my ninth school."

With such frequent upheavals, Byrne faced the challenge of making new friends in every new town they relocated to. Over and over again he found himself in places where "I didn't know anyone and they didn't know me." Although he didn't think of it at the time, later he asked himself, how do people decide who they like and who they don't like among strangers? It was a question that stayed with him through graduate school. In particular, Byrne wondered what the effect of similarity was on nascent relationships.

Let's go back to the two Kellys for a moment. If we were to set them up on a blind date, how likely would it be that they'd hit it off? Could we count on the fact that they share the same name to help bring them together? Or that they both attend church? Or that they're both social and outgoing? How does the adage that opposites attract factor in? Byrne decided to look into these questions through his research.

As Byrne began his investigation into the power of similarity, he faced a major hurdle. As a newly minted Ph.D. at the University of Texas, he had no grant money and no doctoral students. The psychology department could afford to pay for paper and copying, but little else. On top of that, Byrne was a neophyte within academic circles.

As it turned out, however, both of these challenges ended up working to his advantage. Because he was outside the academic loop, Byrne didn't realize that he wasn't the first social psychologist interested in exploring the connection between similarity and attraction. In fact, over the years a number of studies had focused on how similarity affects the likelihood of people forming a relationship. Previous studies, however, had been plagued by a fundamental flaw: they all relied on hypothetical situations. In a typical study, participants were instructed to *pretend* that they had met someone quite similar to them. Perhaps this imagined person had similar physical features or hailed from the same town. The participants were then asked how they would feel about this fictional person. Would they want to become friends? Would they find the person attractive?

The problem with this approach is obvious—asking participants to *guess* how they would react only tells us, at best, what they think they might do. How we *think* we'd respond to a given situation or person is often very different from how we actually do react in real life. Before Byrne came on the scene, no psychologist studying similarity and attraction had come up with a viable way to place subjects in real-life situations—or at least situations that *felt* like real life.

But Byrne hadn't heard about the previous studies. He began his quest unbiased by the inadequate methodology that was then the norm. In fact, his lack of funding forced Byrne to take a rather innovative grassroots approach. Instead of spending money on testing what-if scenarios, Byrne started by interviewing a group of his undergraduate students to find out the topics of interest in their lives. The students told him their attitudes about such things as religion and premarital sex and shared their tastes in music, books, and movies.

The information Byrne gathered proved to be a gold mine, as it reflected what the students actually cared about. Byrne carefully analyzed their responses, identified common themes, and distilled the information down to a list of twenty-six attributes. Half of these were related to the students' attitudes about major life issues, while the other half had to do with taste and everyday preferences.

Next he took a new group of students and presented them with the list of twenty-six attributes, asking them to indicate their agreement or disagreement with each one. For example, a student would indicate whether he or she agreed (or disagreed) with a statement such as "I believe in God" or "I don't really like watching westerns." Their responses gave Byrne a rather comprehensive profile of each student—his or her beliefs, likes, and dislikes.

A few days later, these same students were shown the responses from their counterparts in other classes who had completed the same questionnaire. In order to protect the other students' privacy, the participants were told, the names and identifying information of the other students had been redacted, in a manner similar to that by which classified documents are censored by the government or military.

What the students didn't know, however, was that these "censored" responses were completely fake. The black censor bars didn't really conceal anything at all.

Byrne had, in actuality, created fictional survey responses that mirrored the students' original responses to varying degrees. "They were prepared on my kitchen table," Byrne explained, "with several different pens and pencils of various colors, making check marks and X's, writing large and small, left-handed and right-handed."

He crafted each of the fictional responses so that it would fall into one of four categories. In the first category, Byrne made up responses that exactly matched a specific student's beliefs and attitudes. In other words, the responses were in 100 percent agreement with the student on all twenty-six questions: You believe in God, I believe in God, too. You like jazz music, so do I.

The second category of respondents *disagreed* with the

student on all the issues. So if the original student, for example, indicated that she liked sports, the corresponding fictionalized survey would indicate a dislike of sports, and so on.

For the third category, Byrne created responses in which the fictitious counterpart agreed on the important issues (religion, values) but disagreed on the more trivial ones (taste in music, hobbies). The fourth category was made up of responses in which the counterpart agreed on the unimportant variables but disagreed on the big ones.

A quarter of the original students were given questionnaires in which the fictionalized respondents agreed on all issues, another quarter were given fictionalized questionnaires in which the respondents disagreed on all issues, and so on. Byrne asked each of these separate groups of students to what degree they liked their respective counterparts, based on the questionnaires. Not surprisingly, the students who received surveys that were in total agreement were more likely to think favorably of their counterparts than those who received responses that were in complete disagreement.

But the survey revealed two significant findings. The first was just how much of an effect total agreement had. Students who received questionnaires that were in total agreement (i.e., where the surveys completely mirrored their beliefs and preferences) rated their counterparts 13 out of 14 on an attractiveness scale. Students who received questionnaires that completely disagreed with them gave their counterparts an average score of just 4.41 out 14. That's about as a big a difference as you can find in a social psychology experiment. The participants who received questionnaires that were in total agreement also believed their counterparts to be much more moral, knowledgeable, and intelligent. Not only were they thought to be more attractive, but they were also perceived as better people.

What about the students in the third and fourth categories, whose counterparts shared only half of their characteristics? If we had to guess which factors mattered the most (remember, half the students received responses that were similar in terms of the major issues, and the others received responses that matched only on more minor things such as personal taste), most of us would probably guess that agreement on the major attributes would win out. After all, you'd think that people who share the same religious convictions and political views, for example, would be more likely to hit it off than those who share only similar tastes in films and music.

But the hard data didn't fit this commonsense prediction. It turned out that it didn't matter *at all* which topics underlay the similarity—it was the degree of similarity that was important. "I just couldn't believe it initially," Byrne remembers. Sharing a strong dislike of fast food, for example, was just as powerful a predictor of attraction as favoring the same political party. That is, it wasn't *what* the students agreed on that mattered, it was the *extent* of their agreement.

What's more, in subsequent research Byrne discovered that it doesn't take a huge number of similarities to elicit that attraction. When the experiment was performed with just seven factors (instead of the original twenty-six), they were enough to create the same significant difference in likability.

This brings us back to the two Kellys. Having a similar name was certainly a significant factor that led them to connect. But if they had shared a birthday or just finished reading the same book, the effect might have been equally pronounced.

"One of my first Ph.D.'s had a birthday the same as mine," Byrne told us as he reflected back on his early days at the university, "and someone I knew in college has a birthday the same as mine. And for some reason we all remember that." There's something about similarity, even when it concerns trivial matters, that resonates with us. "It feels good," Byrne says. "In general, you notice when people talk about going to some place—they've been to Italy or whatever—or they went to some restaurant or saw something, and somebody else saw the same thing, they'll say, 'Oh my, isn't it interesting? We both ate at that restaurant.' It's irrelevant, but people like to hear that."

The point is that similarity, no matter what form it takes, leads to greater likability. When we discover a shared similarity with someone we've just met—and as we've seen, it doesn't matter in which areas the similarity occurs—we're more likely to perceive the person as part of what psychologists call an *in-group*. An in-group is a collection of people who share common traits that differentiate them from others. For example, our immediate or extended family is an in-group. We share the same bloodline, the same curly hair or distinctive nose—and also a common history and common experiences. We have a built-in propensity to form close bonds with these individuals because they make up our community: They're the people who care about us, protect us, look after us.

We tend to perceive in-group members in a more favorable light (we think of them as being more attractive and better people). This drive is so strong, so deeply ingrained in us, that casual conversations that reveal similarities naturally trigger the in-group response. A Red Sox fan, for example, naturally forms an in-group with a new acquaintance who happens to be a fellow Red Sox fan. It's easy, from the point of view of a fan, to see other diehards as being more likable.

Would this similarity make you more likely to *behave* differently toward someone? For example, would you be more likely to give up a parking space for someone who was similar to you? Or grant a favor? Or give a loan?

A team of psychologists from Santa Clara University decided to examine the influence of similarity on behavior. They invited a group of women to participate in a study on creativity. (If you're saying to yourself, "I bet the study had nothing to do with creativity," then you've been paying attention. We should note that there's a good reason for the deception. If the participants *knew* that they were involved in a study about similarity, that knowledge couldn't help but change their behavior. It's the same principle that would apply if we were to tell you we were going to measure how many times you blink in a minute. The moment you became aware of your blinking, you'd either overblink or keep your eyes unnaturally still. In fact, just reading about blinking is probably disrupting your natural blinking timing. Sorry about that.) The women had no clue that they were about to take part in an experiment about similarity. The researchers asked each woman to bring a few one-dollar-bills with her to the study. The seemingly odd request would soon prove significant.

When each woman arrived at the lab, she was accompanied by a researcher to a room, where she was asked to empty her pockets and her purse and to place all the items on a table in front of her. The object of the experiment, the woman was told, was to identify different uses for the various personal items on the table. The women were each given five minutes to create as long a list as they could come up with. After completing the task and putting all their personal items back in their purses and pockets, the women were thanked for participating.

It was as they left the lab that the real experiment began. As each woman walked away from the building, she was approached by one of the study researchers, who pretended to be a member of the Cystic Fibrosis Foundation raising money. Remember, the participants had each been instructed to bring one-dollar bills. So the women had small denominations of cash with them. And emptying their pockets and purses had served to remind them that they were carrying those small bills.

When asked to make a donation, many of the participants made a contribution—apparently the women figured that it was a good cause. On average the participants gave exactly one dollar.

The researchers then repeated the experiment, but with a new condition. As before, the women in this study were invited to participate in a creative experiment, instructed to bring dollar bills, and asked to empty their pockets. And just like their counterparts, the women were accosted afterward by a volunteer raising money for cystic fibrosis. The difference was that this time, the woman asking for the donation wore a name tag with the same name as the study participant. If Sally had just left the lab, the Cystic Fibrosis Foundation fund-raiser would happen to be named Sally as well. Kate would meet a fellow Kate, and so on.

It turns out that simply sharing the same name more than doubled the donation amount. Just the flash of a name tag made the participants unconsciously include the fundraiser in their in-group. These women *doubled* the contribution level of the women in the control group and gave, on average, $2.07.

Once we accept people into our in-group, we start seeing them in a different light: we're kinder to them, more generous. And this change in behavior starts a chain re-action. We are much more likely to respond favorably to someone who sees us as part of her in-group. It's much easier to like that person in return.

Business professor J. Brock Smith of the University of Victoria was able to demonstrate how this same force operates in a business setting. He mailed out more than three hundred surveys to members of Canada's Purchasing Management Association and asked them questions about their relationship with a supplier representative with whom they had worked for longer than three months. The sales managers were, by and large, far more committed to those relationships where there was open communication and trust. But the way this feel-good communication and trust was formed goes right back to similarity. The managers weren't necessarily aware of it, but those suppliers whom they most liked also happened to share their attitudes about work and gender. And they also happened to be in a similar place in life, as measured by attributes such as age, marital status, and family situation.

Were the managers drawn by the open communication and trust of the relationship? Or were they instead unconsciously forming in-groups with suppliers who were similar to them?

In a very real way, similarity brings out the best in us. Our tendency to view those within our in-group with a kinder eye gave the two Kelly Hildebrandts a huge head start over the rest of us when they first met. They were members of a two-person in-group from the get-go, making it that much easier to form a connection.

This principle applies as much in gaining favors as it does in love. The same Santa Clara researchers who created the donation experiment conducted another study in which participants were invited to take part in an "astrological" experiment. On the day of the study, each participant walked into a room not knowing what to expect. Shortly after they sat down, another participant arrived (the new person was actually a research associate). The person conducting the experiment told the two participants that the study would measure the claim by astrologers that personality was related to one's birth sign.

Both participants were asked what their birthday was, ostensibly in order to give them the appropriate astrological personality questionnaire. When the person conducting the experiment asked for the research associate's birthday, she gave the same date as the real participant. If a participant was born on, say, February 6, the associate would claim to be born on February 6 as well.

"Not surprisingly," wrote the researchers, "[the participants] typically commented on the coincidence when they gave their answer." But the associate was instructed not to engage in any further conversation with the real participant until after the experiment was over. When the two researchers left the room, their confederate was instructed to ask a favor of the study participant.

Pulling a term paper out of her backpack, she would

tell the participant that she was enrolled in an English class and was required to find a stranger to critique the paper she had written. "I wonder if you could read this eight-page essay for me and give me one page of written feedback on whether my arguments are persuasive and why." The confederate would add apologetically that she needed the critique the next day.

Now, clearly this was asking a lot of the participant. Putting a dollar or two into a jar is one thing. But who wants to read, let alone critique, a fellow student's English paper? Many of us would give more than two dollars just to *avoid* it. It's one of those favors you might ask of a good friend but not of a complete stranger.

In the control condition, when the confederate did not pretend to have the same birthday as the study participant, only a third of the study subjects agreed to comply with the request. But a very different picture emerged when the study subjects thought the person making the critique request had the same birthday—a resounding 62 percent agreed to sacrifice a couple of hours to help out a complete stranger.

The researchers then introduced another variant. This time, they told participants that they and a confederate shared a rare (but completely made up) "type E" fingerprint pattern, found in only 2 percent of the general population. When later asked to critique the English paper, lo and behold, more than 80 percent of the participants agreed to help out.

One could argue that an identical name or similar birthday would suggest a certain shared experience in life, which would help to create a kinship. However, few would have suggested that people would be so generous with their time with a complete stranger as a result of a similarity in the microscopic ridges on their fingertips. But what matters, of course, is our sense of belonging, of a unique common bond. That sense of being part of an in-group. A characteristic shared by only 2 percent of the population is actually a fairly powerful inducement.

In the research studies, the interactions between participants and researchers were all one-offs. The participant and research confederate had no further contact after the study. In real life, however, similarity often leads to a much longer and more involved relationship with the other person. The two Kelly Hildebrandts, after all, fell in love and got married.

Professor Avshalom Caspi, then at the University of Wisconsin–Madison, and his research team from Harvard and the University of California–Riverside studied the relationships of three hundred engaged couples who were mostly in their twenties and thirties. As the studies above would suggest, the couples were much more likely to share similarities—to have things in common—than two people who just happen to meet by coincidence.

The researchers continued to follow the couples over a period of years. Would their level of similarity fade over time? Imagine, for a moment, that you were to walk down the street and bump into your best friend from high school. The two of you might catch up about what was going on in your lives now and reminisce about old teachers and classmates. But if you sat down and talked for an extended period of time, chances are you'd find that you had less in common than you used to—perhaps you'd find that you had diverging outlooks on life or very different interests and hobbies. Over time, people change. Both Kelly Hildebrandts *today* enjoy the outdoors and scuba diving. But how will they feel ten, fifteen, twenty years in the future?

When Caspi and his team looked at the data, however, they discovered something odd. Over the years, although the couples had aged, their levels of similarity had remained unchanged. Twenty years later, their degree of similarity—on everything from religion to politics to their interests in art and music—was the same as ever. They hadn't changed a bit. How could this be?

It comes back to the concept of in-group. The couples were able to maintain their level of similarity through their shared experiences. The significance of a shared fingerprint may diminish after a few weeks. But the experiences of living in the same household and community, raising kids together, going through the ups and downs of life together, maintains the sense of being part of an in-group that helped to create the bond in the first place.

At its core, each of the accelerators we've discussed works to break down that invisible barrier all of us have when walking down a crowded street or meeting a new person. Vulnerability helps to allow others into our lives while laying bare who we are. Physical proximity—even if we're not aware of it—encourages us to see the people around us as individuals rather than strangers. Physical closeness fosters emotional closeness. Resonance—connecting with those around us—encourages us to share that experience. In turn, we start seeing others in a different light. And similarity helps to foster or facilitate a connection between two people, as relative strangers are seen as part of our in-group.

One thing we haven't looked at is the broader environment in which the click accelerators operate. Are we more likely, for example, to click with another person or become fully engaged with the world around us while sitting on the beach or while waiting in a line at the movie theater? Why do certain situations—such as the first day or week of college—seem to engender quick-set intimacy?

In the next chapter, we're going to look at the role our environment plays in shaping our interactions with the world and with those around us.

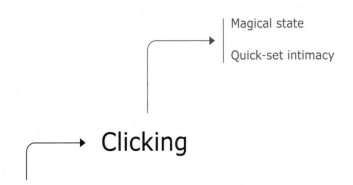

Magical state

Quick-set intimacy

Clicking

Click Accelerators

Vulnerability

Transactional
- Phatic
- Factual
- Evaluative

Connective
- Gut-level
- Peak

Proximity

Exponential Attraction
- Spontaneous communications
- Passive contacts

Resonance

Flow

Presence
- Intentionality
- Mutuality
- Individuality
- Attentiveness

Similarity

Quantity over quality

In-group

Long-lasting effect

CHAPTER 6

Fire, Combat, and Nathan's Living Room: The Role of Place

We met Fred Wahpepah, a Native American elder from the Kickapoo and Sac-and-Fox tribes, in an Italian restaurant in an El Cerrito, California, mall. Wahpepah, wearing a turquoise necklace and a long ponytail, had grown up in Oklahoma and served in the Korean War. It was when he was working as a veteran in the Oakland shipyards that he rediscovered his native roots.

"There are so many sidewalk Indians wandering about," he told us, referring to tribe members who've spent the bulk of their lives away from traditional ways—trading dirt paths in favor of paved sidewalks. Wahpepah tells us he was "one of them."

Now seventy-nine, Wahpepah, for the past thirty years, has reembraced his roots, leading sweat lodge ceremonies for Native Americans and the general public nearly every weekend. The sweat lodge ceremonies he conducts have been practiced by tribes including the Navajo, Naskapi, and Cree since well before Columbus arrived in America.

"You don't have to have my heritage to join. You can be religious, or not religious at all," he said with a smile. "You just need an openness to participate and honor the tradition."

During a sweat lodge ceremony, the group steps inside a half-dome structure made of bent wood covered with heavy blankets. The dome is constructed in such a way that very little light can get in. Just outside the dome a fire pit is used to heat up rocks. When these are hot, the sweat leader—the person conducting the ceremony—places them inside the lodge and pours water over them to create steam. "It is a very important job," he tells us. The sweat leader holds "the sacred space."

The sweats are done in sequence—the group sits for about thirty minutes before the doors are opened briefly, and then the next round begins. The heat is intense. It is not uncommon for people to feel physically drained to the point of exhaustion. Yet there is something about the atmosphere that more than makes up for the physical discomfort. The sweat lodge ceremony has been used for centuries by indigenous people for physical cleansing, medicinal purposes, and spiritual growth. Another equally powerful side effect is the intense connection it helps to form among the group members.

"Not too long ago," Wahpepah told us, "a good friend of mine came to a ceremony and he met a woman there."

The two hadn't known each other beforehand, but peering at each other across the circle, they felt an immediate attraction. Afterward they got acquainted. "We could all see how strong their connection was. Within twenty-four hours they were engaged—boom—like that."

Was there something about Wahpepah's ceremony that helped to bring about such a powerful personal connection? It's not the kind of environment one would think would foster love at first sight—nor is it designed to do so. Still, certain aspects of the "sacred space," as Wahpepah referred to the sweat lodge surroundings, do seem to play a significant role in inducing quick-set intimacy. It is here that we find our fifth click accelerator: the environmental factors that play a part in creating an instant connection, or click, between people.

The way Wahpepah's sweat lodge ceremony works to bring people together sheds new light on a conundrum posed in a study written by psychiatrist Gerald Klerman and psychologist Myrna Weissman and published in the *Journal of the American Medical Association*. Klerman and Weissman noticed an unusual phenomenon in the decades after World War II. In industrialized countries such as the United States, Sweden, Germany, Canada, and New Zealand, rates of depression increased at an alarming rate, while in other places, such as South Korea and Puerto Rico, they remained stable.

Statistical analysis by other experts confirmed Klerman and Weissman's observations. Not only were the rates of depression in certain industrialized countries climbing exponentially, but people were beginning to exhibit symptoms of depression at a younger age. This disturbing phenomenon was especially surprising given that the standard of living in the decades after World War II in Western industrialized countries was rising; people were better off and living more comfortably in terms of material goods than at any other time in history.

By 1956, the majority of Americans held white-collar jobs, as opposed to lower-paying blue-collar jobs. Child mortality rates were decreasing, and access to modern health care and nutritious food was on the rise. People faced less physical discomfort, were healthier and lived longer, and enjoyed the benefits of an explosion of new technology.

The contrast between life in the industrialized nations and life in third-world countries was stark. Let's take a look, for instance, at the average American man in 1960 and his South Korean counterpart. The American enjoyed an income of $13,414, while the South Korean earned less than a tenth of that amount. In America, there were 400 cars for every 1,000 people, compared with only 1 car per 1,000 people in Korea. Infant mortality rates in South Korea were three times worse than in the United States. Life expectancy was a mere fifty-five years, compared with seventy years in the United States.

Nonetheless, for some reason, South Koreans as a population were significantly less depressed than Americans. More surprising, however, is what has happened to the rates of depression in South Korea in the years since 1960. Over the following decades, the Korean economy enjoyed substantial growth, and today the standard of living in Korea is much higher than it was fifty years ago. There are now 293 cars for every 1,000 people. Infant mortality and life expectancy have improved so much that they have surpassed the corresponding levels in the United States. South Korea has an infant mortality rate of 4.1 per 1,000 live births, compared with 6.3 per 1,000 live births in America. Life expectancy has climbed to seventy-nine years in South Korea; in the United States, it is seventy-eight.

Based on the numbers, the South Koreans are doing extraordinarily well. And yet, with all the economic improvements, the suicide rate in South Korea soared to 24.7 per 100,000 people in 2005. That's an extraordinary increase—in 1985, just twenty years earlier, the rate was only 9.1 per 100,000 people. In other words, the suicide rate nearly tripled, even as Koreans were enjoying a much higher standard of living.

What had changed in Korea over the last decades? The sentiments of one contributor to a South Korean online discussion forum reflect those of too many people in the country: "Most of all," the writer said, "I don't know why I should exist. I don't think I'm worth anything. Nobody will care if I die . . . even my parents. I should just die. Can someone please tell me a perfect way to commit suicide?"

What is even more disturbing about this post is that it was written by a sixth grader.

As South Korea has become more industrialized, the country has followed the same pattern that Klerman and Weissman observed earlier in industrialized Western countries. In country after country, when a society becomes industrialized, depression and suicide rates shoot up. Something about the process of industrialization is making people very unhappy.

The cause of the increased levels of depression may not be industrialization in and of itself. That is, it seems unlikely that a new washing machine in the house necessarily makes a family more depressed. Nonetheless, the relationship between industrialization and depression is so strong that scientists know there is *some* correlation between the two. What is it about the process of a country becoming industrialized that leads to depression?

In order to tackle this question, it is important to compare like with like. South Korea and the United States are very different culturally—industrialized or not. And for that matter, South Korea in 1960 bears little resemblance to South Korea in the twenty-first century. Because countries have such complex social systems, it's difficult to isolate a specific cause or factor contributing to depression. But as it turns out, the same trend that we saw among industrialized countries can also be seen among different industries within the same country.

A highly industrialized country such as Japan is actually made up of both the industrialized, high-tech sectors we tend to associate with the Japanese economy and more traditional sectors, where individuals perform what can be thought of as preindustrial tasks. This duality gave researchers at Japan's Jichi Medical School a chance to observe two groups of people living in the same country, abiding by the same cultural norms, sharing a similar cultural history. One group worked in white-collar industrial jobs (such as office work, management, and technical work) and the other worked in more traditional, blue-collar professions (such as farming and skilled manual labor). Although both groups lived in the same country during the same time period, a familiar pattern emerged. The industrialized workers were substantially more prone to suffer from depression than the group that performed manual labor.

Think about what it's like for the more depressed, white-collar group. In a way, postindustrialized life is the opposite of Wahpepah's sweat lodge ceremony. In a sweat lodge, you sit side by side with others, sharing stories, enduring the heat and humidity of the sweat lodge together; throughout the ceremony, you're a part of a close-knit group. Compare that with spending a day in an air-conditioned office, working alone in your cubicle at your computer, interacting with few people. Moreover, at the end of the day, you tend to go home to watch TV alone or with your family.

We know that our social environment plays a signifi-cant role in our sense of well-being. And that is the crux of our fifth click accelerator. The environmental factors that keep members of a population connected with one another and psychologically healthy are the same factors that con-tribute to two people clicking with each other.

Let's take a closer look at the opposite of today's in-dustrialized society, the sweat lodge ceremony. The partici-pants sit in an extremely hot, enclosed space, surrounded by other people who are enduring the same uncomfort-able conditions. That shared adversity, that sense of going through something difficult together, serves to bring peo-ple together in a unique and powerful way.

In preindustrialized societies, everyday life was, by nearly all measures, filled with greater hardships than we experience today. Parents were more likely to lose a child; people often did not have enough to eat, and they were more likely to die from disease. They were subjected to harsher work conditions and managed without electricity or running water in their homes. And yet this shared ad-versity served to bring people in the community together.

Think about how many times you have reached out to another person with small talk by complaining about work or the weather or the economy—an overture that may have ultimately led to a friendship or deeper relationship. Think about the bond that is created when students, for example, pull an all-nighter together studying for a final, or when colleagues band together against a terrible boss, or when travelers are stuck at an airport for hours awaiting a delayed flight.

Most adversity is thrust upon us. But sometimes we deliberately seek it out, as when we go on an Outward Bound wilderness adventure. The personal growth and bonding that people experience through Outward Bound are also the purpose behind wilderness camps for troubled teens.

John Karren, admissions director at Utah's Elements Wilderness Program, a camp for teenage boys with behavioral problems, points to the advantages of having kids face a strange, challenging environment together. "For us it's getting the kids out of their normal environment. Getting the kids away from electronics—all these different things that they have that are so readily available." At camp, the kids have no video games, no access to fast food, no TV, and no text messages to distract or entertain them.

At first the change is a shock. "We hike two to five miles every day," Karren says. For many of the teens, this is the first time they've had to do strenuous exercise. "There's definitely something about being in the wilderness, something about sitting around a campfire at night when it's dark or looking up and seeing the starry sky [that brings kids together]. Making your own fire, cooking your meals."

In these types of programs, hiking and cooking their own food help to create a sense of kinship and camaraderie among the teens. We would argue that the campers bond together *because* the program is so challenging and demanding. Sandra Jo Wilson and Mark W. Lipsey of Van-derbilt University pinpoint two factors that help to predict a wilderness camp's success rate among kids with behavioral problems. The first, continual sessions of psychotherapy, makes sense in a camp for kids with behavior problems. But the second factor Wilson and Lipsey identify—the one that comes up again and again in nearly every successful program—applies to everyone. It involves exposing the kids to a challenging physical environment that includes long hikes and spartan living conditions. In other words, it involves enduring adversity together: suffering through blisters, nagging insects, fatigue, or exhaustion. The kids band together like soldiers battling a common enemy.

This concept of shared adversity is a key factor in bring-ing people together, and it has always been a strong com-ponent of Navajo society. A youth program in New Mexico called Alchini Binitsekees Nahalzhooh (which translates to "Restoring the Children's Thinking Back to Harmony"), in fact, invited troubled teens to participate in—you guessed it—sweat lodge ceremonies. As hot steam rose from the water poured over the rocks, these teens reflected on their pasts and talked candidly about their hopes and fears. Their shared experiences helped the kids to be more open with one another. They bragged about their ability to en-dure the heat. During the last round, they asked the leader to bring in the maximum number of hot rocks so that they could claim they had endured the worst the sweat lodge had to offer.

Enduring adversity together creates an intense shared emotional experience. It reduces the emotional barriers we naturally put up to safeguard ourselves and creates a sense of camaraderie among those of us who have gone through the process together.

Do the connections formed in the midst of a challenging situation have long-lasting effects, however? Can the experience permanently affect the relationships of those involved? A growing body of research suggests that the greater the intensity of the adversity, the stronger the bond that is established between the participants afterward. Glen H. Elder Jr. of the University of North Carolina at Chapel Hill and Elizabeth C. Clipp of Duke University conducted a longitudinal study of veterans who served in various branches of the U.S. military during World War II and the Korean War. It's one thing to complete a long, strenuous hike together or spend an hour or two in a sweat lodge; it's another to serve together in combat, where your very life is at risk. Elder and Clipp scrutinized a mountain of data that tracked these veterans for forty years, from the time they joined the military to their golden years as senior citizens.

Regardless of which branch they served in, the men in the study fell into one of three categories—those who saw no combat, those who participated in combat but had no exposure to death, and those who participated in combat and were exposed to death. The interviews and data revealed that the more intense the battle conditions, the

stronger the camaraderie that developed among the soldiers. Not surprisingly, they tended to form a firmer bond
with a comrade they had fought with side by side than with
a buddy they had worked with in the mess hall. Elder and
Clipp wanted to find out how long such ties would last.

One simple indicator of the strength of the relationship was the number of friends the veterans had from their
service days. Elder and Clipp found that the veterans who
experienced deadly combat were nearly twice as likely to
maintain friendships with their fellow battalion members
as were the veterans who weren't directly exposed to death.
They were also twice as likely to attend reunions of war
buddies. "The most painful loss is the death of a comrade,
and yet that experience is coupled with the highest preva-
lence of enduring friendships from the service," explained
Elder and Clipp. Adjustments for differences in education
and extroversion did not alter the findings.

The experience of men facing life-or-death situations together created unbreakable bonds. In other words, it didn't
matter what type of person went into combat—simply the
fact that they faced combat together made the soldiers'
bond stronger. It is one of the most emotionally charged
experiences imaginable.

Whether by design or by happenstance, the "hot rocks
in the sweat lodge"—that shared sense of adversity—plays
a critical role in shaping the intensity of the relationship
among those involved. But that intense bonding involves
more than just shared adversity. Using the sweat lodge

example, it's important that the participants were together inside the lodge as well. "We're all one when we sit in the circle," Wahpepah explained to us. "In a lecture room you see everybody's heads; in a circle you see everybody. You're making a connection because you're seeing each other's expressions. When they're sharing, a lot of people get emotional. They cry like babies. There's power in that circle."

Sitting together inside the lodge is so powerful because the sweat lodge creates a very clear physical boundary between the "community" inside the lodge and the outside world. Psychologists call this boundary a frame; it is a clear delineation of an event or a relationship.

A clearly defined or "framed" community is the second environmental factor that encourages a click. Inside the half dome of the sweat lodge, the outside world is excluded. Little external light comes in. You're alone with the rest of the group, cut off from the outside world. Everything that takes place is unique to the group. There's no question who's a part of the group and who isn't.

Think about a time you've clicked with someone. Can you remember the environment in which that connection occurred? Take, for example, a student on his or her first day of college. Essentially he or she is leaving behind one world and entering a well-defined new community. The frame is clear. You know who's part of the community (the other students and professors on the campus), what its borders are, and what defines it. There is even often an us-versus-them sentiment between those attending the college and those who live in the surrounding community.

In 1984, we both experienced this phenomenon for ourselves, growing up. Our family had moved from Tel Aviv, Israel, to El Paso, Texas. On our second day in town, before we had even had a chance to fully unpack, we were summoned to the unofficial Israeli embassy in El Paso—the house of Nathan and his wife, Shoshana, teachers at the local Hebrew school. Their house was always open to visitors, and families never had to call ahead to drop by. Everyone seemed to congregate at Nathan's; he and his wife never seemed to leave the house.

Stepping inside Nathan and Shoshana's house, we were transported from the southwestern desert back to Tel Aviv. The living room was dominated by a red shag carpet; the couches formed a rectangle around a coffee table. There were always snacks laid out for visitors. Conversations varied from cultural reflections on El Paso to discussions of politics and current events to memories of personal life experiences. As kids, sitting on one of the big couches, reaching over to grab a handful of pretzel sticks, we felt like we had been dropped into an entirely different universe—not quite Israel, but definitely not El Paso.

In a way, Nathan's house felt a lot like the inside of Wahpepah's sweat lodge: you became part of an instant community that was very different from the world outside. On that first visit, our parents hit it off with friends they're still in touch with today, decades later. What made Nathan's house special wasn't just Nathan's hospitality or the fact that we met fellow Israelis; it was more the fact that we were part of a "club," Nathan's club. We found his house a natural place to form deep connections with other visitors. One way that such defined communities foster clicking is by giving the people who are members permission to let their guard down and to embrace one another as members of the same clan or tribe.

This kind of frame, or defined community, reinforces the earlier accelerators we've explored. Spending time together in close quarters, of course, triggers the proximity response. Being a part of the same community helps to create a sense of being part of an in-group. Feeling safe together and experiencing adversity together both help to make one more open and willing to be vulnerable.

The frame, in other words, helps to amplify the other accelerators. It is something that Tel Aviv University professor Naama Sabar explored at length in her investigation of Israel's kibbutz community. The kibbutz movement in Israel started as an idealized version of Zionism. But by the 1990s, many kibbutz members had become disillusioned; in fact, they were twice as likely as their city counterparts to migrate out of Israel altogether.

What happened to these kibbutz members—or kibbutzniks—when they left the country, Sabar wondered? After all, it's not an easy transition to make. "In Israel," explains Sabar, "the term for emigration is *yerida*, a word that literally means 'descent' and suggests a descent from a high place (Israel) to a low place (the Diaspora)."

Sabar followed a large set of former kibbutzniks to the San Fernando Valley in Los Angeles. Though they had lived in very different kibbutzes back in Israel, they were now all residing in the same general geographical region. In fact, they seemed to be drawn to one another.

Here is the story of one such kibbutznik, a young man named Alon. When Alon first arrived in the United States, "he was picked up at the airport by Arik [a fellow ex-kibbutznik]," Sabar recounts. "On the way to Arik's apartment, they went to the local Motor Vehicles Bureau. Alon passed the written driving test by filling in a form in Hebrew, with Arik signaling hints to the answers." From the DMV, the pair continued straight to several used car lots—all run by Israeli immigrants—and discussed Alon's new job, again, working for Israelis. "Thus, at the end of his first day in the United States," Sabar mused, "Alon had a California driving license, a car, and a job that had been arranged for him prior to his arrival—all with minimal English." On his first night in America, Alon was visited by "old-timers" in the community who gave him advice about how to get along in this new environment. The kibbutz members had left the commune lifestyle to seek privacy and independence, yet ironically, they ended up forming an unofficial and informal kibbutz in Los Angeles, thousands of miles from Israel.

Sabar called the community Kibbutz LA. If you were

to attend a gathering, through the haze of cigarette smoke—one common practice was chain smoking—you'd find everyone dressed in informal kibbutz attire, eating refreshments that easily could have come out of a kibbutz dining hall, speaking in a distinct Israeli dialect that other Israelis would have a difficult time understanding. "Paradoxically," wrote Sabar, "although 85 percent of the interviewees mentioned the search for anonymity and privacy as a reason for leaving the kibbutz, in Los Angeles, they sought one another out."

But from the perspective of how we click, or form instant connections, the dynamic isn't so surprising. Yes, in many ways life on the Israeli kibbutz was difficult. It makes sense that people would want to seek out a more comfortable and prosperous future for themselves. But when they left the kibbutz, they were still hungry for that sense of a defined community, or frame, and the intimacy that it engendered. Certainly, Kibbutz LA offered members the benefits of social networking—jobs, cars, useful tips on where to go shopping. But on a more important, emotional level, it created a group of people who bonded with one another, much the same way that the military veterans who endured combat together bonded.

Because it was largely self-contained, the community provided the emotional support its members needed. One member, for example, comforted a new arrival: "Don't worry, Dvorka, I was down in the dumps too at first, nearly everyone is, but afterwards somehow I learned to look on the bright side. . . . If it weren't for these great guys here, I wouldn't have been able to stick it out."

What's interesting is that within the protected frame of Kibbutz LA, the members spent a lot of their time kvetching about their present circumstances. The United States wasn't safe enough. Los Angeles didn't feel like home. They didn't want to raise their children there. And most of all, they missed their lives in Israel. Kibbutz LA didn't just provide a clearly delineated community; it also was a place to share their feelings about their shared adversity. And that was a magnet that drew members closer to one another. Kibbutz members were able to let down their hair, so to speak, while facing the challenges of a new country. That sense of emotional safety plays a pivotal role in the sweat lodge as well. It can turn the experience of a bunch of strangers sitting together in a sauna into a deeply meaningful event, where participants can express themselves candidly in ways that would be considered odd or ill-advised outside the bounds of the community.

The sweat lodge and Kibbutz LA are representative of a much larger human need—to be a part of something larger than oneself, to connect in a meaningful way with the larger world. It is something all of us yearn for, consciously or not, from office workers to executives in the corner office.

After 9/11, Ori became involved in helping CEOs who wanted to contribute to the community or country in light of the attacks. The executives came from very different backgrounds and regions, and the challenge was how to make this disparate group of executives gel. All of the CEOs were dedicated to and passionate about making the program work. But it was a new venture for everyone involved, and no one quite knew how to go about it. Add to that mix the CEOs' background in managing others and commanding from on high, and it seemed a recipe for disaster.

Ori decided to create a frame, or defined community, that was wholly different from what the CEOs were used to. For starters, he made the environment as non-business-like as possible: no cell phones in the room, no PowerPoint presentations. There were no specific agendas or to-do lists. Rather than a conference room, the group met at a hotel suite. The atmosphere was purposely intimate, relaxed, and—most important—separate from the participants' everyday lives.

To create a safe environment, Ori asked the members to introduce themselves to each other by describing the single best and single worst moments in their lives. He wanted to make it clear that the meeting wasn't about proving one's leadership abilities but about connecting with one another on a human level.

And as a result, the CEOs opened up. Recalling their best times was easy enough: the day their company went public, the day their first child was born, or the day they were featured in a glowing newspaper or magazine article.

But asking about their *worst* day proved to be the turning point of the meeting. If someone asked you out of the blue to describe your worst day ever, the real question is, do you trust the group—do you trust the frame—enough to be completely candid and honest?

Ori wasn't sure whether the CEOs would be willing to get that personal—whether they felt safe enough in that shared space. But the corporate heads surprised him. They talked candidly about everything from difficult family relationships to personal regrets. Some became emotional and teary-eyed. By the afternoon of the first day, the emotional space they had created had captured the same sense of safety and trust that the members of Kibbutz LA experienced. It changed the dynamic of the group from one of overachieving intellectuals to one of committed individuals who trusted one another on the deepest emotional level.

"You know," one of the participants said, turning to a counterpart sitting next to him, "I never thought I'd feel this close to you. But I just feel like I know you, like I get you, beyond just business interactions."

The first of these "circles" that Ori helped to put together was so powerful that some of the CEOs decided to start their own groups. In those groups, too, the goal was to create a safe environment and minimize formal presentations and flow charts in favor of shared stories. The camaraderie these circles built was profound. And as a result, some of the groups achieved remarkable results—helping to open up borders between hostile countries in South Asia or raising funds for relief efforts in Africa. But it all started with the deep bond created among the members.

Those common bonds and that sense of community don't just foster instant connections—they help to make for happier individuals. Despite the gap in depression rates between industrialized and nonindustrialized workers, there are clear examples of industrialized workplaces producing happy, fulfilled employees. The secret, however, isn't lavish bonuses or other perks. A Finnish health survey conducted on thousands of employees from 2000 to 2003 revealed that those employees who had experienced a genuine sense of community at work were healthier psychologically. Workers who felt supported by their supervisor and coworkers were significantly less likely to exhibit symptoms of depression. They were also less likely to take antidepressants.

The big takeaway here is that there are changes we can embrace to create a healthier work environment—and that facing adverse conditions can actually be an opportunity for a company to improve morale and create a closer-knit workforce. Perhaps those corporate survival retreats are more than just a frivolous perk. While we can't re-create a half-dome sweat lodge in the workplace, companies *can* look for ways to foster a sense of a framed community.

Each of the accelerators we've looked at—vulnerability, proximity, resonance, similarity, and environment—offers an opportunity to bring people together in a fuller, richer way. We can allow ourselves to become more vulnerable to others; we can place greater emphasis on bringing people in teams and departments together. We can strive to be more present in our day-to-day activities; and we can work to create an environment that is more cohesive and has a greater sense of community. But are there people for whom all of this is second nature? In the next chapter we'll investigate whether some people are simply more prone to form instant connections.

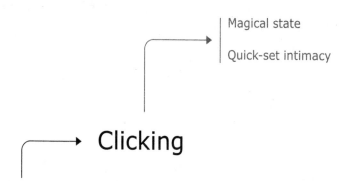

Clicking

Click Accelerators

Vulnerability

Transactional
- Phatic
- Factual
- Evaluative

Connective
- Gut-level
- Peak

Proximity

Exponential Attraction
- Spontaneous communications
- Passive contacts

Resonance

Flow

Presence
- Intentionality
- Mutuality
- Individuality
- Attentiveness

Similarity

Quantity over quality

In-group

Long-lasting effect

Safe Place

Joint adversity

Frame

CHAPTER 7

Naturals

Come early spring, Dina Kaplan's mailbox starts filling up with wedding invitations, many more events than most of us would be able to attend. The thirtysomething entrepreneur, who runs an online media company in New York, receives invitations from lifelong friends, but a staggering number are from people Kaplan has known for a very short period of time—individuals she's met once or twice at cocktail parties.

The stream of invitations is invigorating for Kaplan, and she's often juggling three or four social engagements in one night. At an event, she moves with ease from one person to another, connecting quickly yet meaningfully with the majority of the people she meets. It can make one's head spin to watch her. What's especially striking is how varied her social interactions are: she makes friends with a photographer, engages in a long conversation with a producer, makes plans to meet for coffee with a human resources manager to whom she's introduced herself.

"What ends up happening," she told us, describing herself at a social event, "is that there is this sort of magical moment when you connect with someone. Even though it's a busy party or conference, with two hundred other people there, you know you are going to stay in touch. Possibly for decades. You know it, they know it. You don't even have to say anything or talk about it. You both just know that in this moment of friendship, chemistry has taken place. It happens all the time."

It happens all the time? Perhaps she's been going to different events than most of us. We doubt that many people instantly click like that with so many others on a regular basis. Think back to the individuals you've met in the past year. Most of us would be able to count the occurrences of a genuine, lasting relationship growing out of such a casual contact on one hand. We asked Kaplan how she was able to form so many rapid, meaningful connections with others. She looked genuinely puzzled. "I thought this was normal for everyone.

"It's a little bit like cosmic fairy dust," Kaplan explained. "I want to go and hang out with that person and get to know them better." During our conversation, Kaplan kept saying, "Don't make me appear as if I'm someone special." When it comes down to it, though, there *is* something special about her. Someone with Kaplan's unique ability to connect with others is rare; we wanted to get a better understanding of that "cosmic fairy dust."

Throughout the book, we've looked at a number of factors that can accelerate our ability to click with an event or activity or another person. Some people, however, are just better at forming quick-set intimacy, and Kaplan is one of them. Yes, she is definitely friendly, charismatic, and attractive. It's tempting to believe that her physical appearance and extroverted personality draw people to her. While it's true that those factors play a role in shaping people's perception, we've all met attractive and outgoing men or women who don't necessarily engender a magical response.

Neal Hamil, head of Elite Model Management's North American division, is someone who has extensive experience observing how beautiful women affect those around them. Elite's list of current and past clients includes the likes of Tyra Banks, Gisele Bundchen, Cindy Crawford, Heidi Klum, and Paulina Porizkova. Hamil himself is credited with developing such supermodels as Naomi Campbell.

Hamil is always on the lookout for new talent. It was late August, just before the semiannual Fashion Week in New York's Bryant Park, when we caught up with him. He was so much in demand that he was actually hiding from his staff. "It's completely crazy here right now," he told us. "I tried to sneak away to find a quiet corner to talk with you, but they know where to find me."

During the week, the world's top fashion houses showcase new trends for the upcoming season. There's a mass pilgrimage to New York—with journalists, models, and everyone who's anyone in the fashion world (and their friends) descending upon the city. You could fill several sports arenas with would-be models who dream of being on the runway during Fashion Week. Hamil, though, has developed a well-trained instinct about what it takes to actually get there. "Beauty is beauty," he told us matter-of-factly, dismissing the biggest misconception about the modeling world—that a model's success is based entirely on her looks. "The models wouldn't be in our office if they weren't tall and gorgeous with long legs and amazing bodies. What puts models over is personality."

Essentially, once you reach the highest levels of the modeling world, beauty is just a prerequisite. The extra oomph—a personality that makes a model click with the camera and with those around her—is essential for someone like Hamil. It is the difference between representing an extraordinarily beautiful woman who can successfully strut down the catwalk and representing an extraordinarily beautiful woman who can serve as the representative of a fragrance or a high-end cosmetics line. That's where real success lies in the industry—being selected as the face of a brand.

"Just earlier this morning," Hamil said, giving us an example of how much a certain type of personality matters, "this girl arrived from Brazil. This is her first time in New York. I'd never met her. I'd only seen her pictures. And now here she was: smiling, beaming, 'Hello! Hi!' She had it."

At the Elite offices, where encountering a stunningly

gorgeous woman is commonplace, when a model comes in with a Dina Kaplan personality, the agents can't help but take notice. "The model today, she was saying hello to every single person in the office," Hamil recalled, "and automatically every agent here, the next phone call they took was, 'Oh my God, you have to meet this great girl who just got here from Brazil! She's fabulous! Go on the Web site. You've got to meet her, she's really fun, she's really sweet.'"

Of course, the modeling world is very different from the high-tech world Dina Kaplan travels in. But the qualities that make someone click are the same. "I've seen a girl's personality completely turn a client on to the point where she swings the whole thing in her favor," says Hamil. "As a model, you have to be warm, friendly, and comfortable meeting strangers."

It's a quality that doesn't necessarily come across in a portfolio. But the moment Hamil meets a model who clicks in person, he discerns a categorical difference. "It's magical," he said. "Our staff might have had another model in mind to pitch to someone for a project, and all of a sudden—boom—there is a girl they know will make them look good to the people they're sending her out to meet. She's going to have a greater chance of getting the job."

What is it about certain people that makes it so easy to connect with them? Why do we want to invite them to our wedding after only a few conversations? The answer to these questions lies in the resolution to a psychological debate that raged in the halls of academia for the better part of a century.

At the heart of the debate is the question of whether personality actually exists. One camp, the personality theorists, believed that personality shapes all our behaviors. A man who has an impulsive personality will make rash decisions when interacting with his family, coworkers, friends, and new acquaintances. But other psychologists contended that personality didn't actually exist—that our actions were learned behaviors akin to a dog learning to salivate at the sound of a bell. Just because we act impulsively when it comes to eating chocolate cake, they argued, doesn't mean we will make impulsive decisions in another context—say, personal finance.

Are we an expression of our innate personalities or a collection of learned behavioral responses? The debate hinged on a fundamental question—do we have a psyche and a core self that drives our actions, or are we born as empty vessels to be filled with a repertoire of conditioned responses?

In dozens of experiments, psychologists measured a given subject's propensity toward generosity, optimism, introversion, creativity, impulsivity, or aggression. They then monitored subjects as they confronted real-life situations. If the personality side of the debate was right, the subjects should be expected to always act in accordance with their innate traits. Generous people would tend to act generously, and optimistic individuals would see the glass as half full. Likewise, if the behavioral-response camp was right, there should be little correlation between how one scores on a personality test and how one behaves in real life.

The experiment results, however, left both sides scratching their heads. Personality appeared to dictate behavior, but only some of the time. Going back to our impulsivity example, people scoring high on impulsivity did indeed act more impulsively. But here was the catch: in some situations they acted very deliberately. Conversely, patient people sometimes acted impulsively when their psychological buttons were pushed. Personality mattered, it seemed, but only to a degree. Likewise, social contexts affected behavior but didn't dictate it. Something wasn't adding up.

Stanford University doctoral candidate Mark Snyder realized that both sides were missing a key piece of the puzzle. What all the experts had failed to consider is that some people's personalities are more fluid than others'. Let's say two women score exactly the same on a personality test measuring optimism. They both feel the future will bring good things. One woman brings that perspective, those traits, to every new situation. She's optimistic at work, optimistic with friends, and optimistic when investing in stocks. The second woman—the one with a more fluid personality—instinctively assesses the social situation and modulates her optimism accordingly. If there are layoffs at work, her natural optimism will give way to uneasiness or dread, matching the feelings of the people around her. In other words, as she goes from situation to situation she picks up on social cues about how appropriate a particular demeanor or behavior might be.

Snyder reasoned, "Some individuals have learned that their affective experience and expression are either socially inappropriate or lacking. Such people may *monitor* (observe and control) their self-presentation and expressive behavior." In other words, some people are more prone to pick up on social cues and adjust how they act and how they are perceived by others. This distinction helps to explain why Dina Kaplan is so easy to connect with. Snyder called people like Kaplan and the Brazilian model *high self-monitors*.

Most of us lie somewhere along a continuum in terms of self-monitoring. Imagine you're in a romantic restaurant where couples talk in hushed voices around candlelit tables. Someone who is a low self-monitor likely will be less successful at modulating his voice to fit the environment. He may use the same tone he'd use at work, not realizing he's talking louder than anyone else in the restaurant. A high self-monitor, on the other hand, won't just modulate his voice; he'll pick up on the emotional temperature of the restaurant and his dining partner and match it perfectly.

When most of us meet a new person, we typically spend a great deal of energy trying to find common ground. Without thinking about it, as we talk to the other person, we're also evaluating whether we're coming across in the right way, whether we're talking too much or too little, whether we're being too formal or too flippant.

A high self-monitor does all the work for us. Rather than trying to find common ground, he or she will meet us where we are. If we're feeling excited and ebullient, the high self-monitor will act ebullient and energetic as well. If we're reflective and serious, he or she will join us in being quiet and introspective. High self-monitors don't simply mirror our actions and behaviors; they complement them. Have you ever been in a conversation with someone and somehow known exactly the right thing to say? That's how high self-monitors lead their lives every day.

Although high self-monitors modulate their behavior to fit the situation, they are not being fraudulent—they are actually just as genuine and principled as everyone else. They don't toss their values or genuine selves aside; they just know what behaviors the situation or the environment calls for in order for the other person to feel comfortable and valued. Reflects Dina Kaplan, "In business situations, I try to be as non-robotic as possible, not to give someone a canned pitch. Mostly, I try to talk to someone as a peer." The reason most of us are more likely to click with someone who is a high self-monitor is that they allow us to be ourselves around them. "It all happens organically," Kaplan continued. "It's never practiced."

Mark Snyder developed a scale to measure an individual's level of self-monitoring. Low self-monitors tended to agree with statements such as "I find it hard to imitate the behavior of other people" and "I have trouble changing my behavior to suit different people and different situations." High self-monitors, on the other hand, resonate with statements like "I can make impromptu speeches even on topics about which I have almost no information."

When Snyder studied high self-monitors, conducting in-depth interviews with the people in their respective social circles, he found that high self-monitors possessed several distinct attributes. First, they had an unusual ability to modulate their emotional expression, which made them extremely adept at picking up on social cues. Second, high self-monitors quickly learned what behaviors were appropriate in various situations. Finally, they were able to easily manage the perceptions of others.

With these telltale attributes in mind, it becomes easy to spot a high self-monitor. A little while ago, the two of us were traveling on a Delta Airlines flight from San Francisco to Atlanta. One of the flight attendants, a woman named Maia Andrade, asked Rom about his drink selection, and, picking up a hint of an accent, inquired, "Where are you from?"

When Rom answered, "Israel," Andrade responded, *"Ma nishma?"*—Hebrew for "How are you?"—and proceeded to hand Rom a plastic cup of ice along with a can of the apple-cranberry juice he'd ordered. Ori, meanwhile, was working on his laptop, oblivious to the conversation. Suddenly he looked up and saw that Rom had been given an entire can of juice (instead of the usual half-filled cup).

Pointing at Rom's tray table, Ori asked Rom in Hebrew, "What, she gave you the whole can?" Without missing a beat, Andrade put her hands in the air, perfectly mimicking a common Israeli hand gesture, and announced, *"Lamah lo? Lamah lo?"*—"Why not? Why not?"

Andrade wasn't overly friendly or gregarious. But she instinctively knew to be gregarious around *us*. A couple of rows later, she encountered a young mother holding a crying baby. Effortlessly, Andrade changed her demeanor, speaking in hushed, comforting tones to the baby, who immediately stopped crying. Andrade then went on to commiserate with the mother about the challenges of traveling with an infant. A few rows further on, the flight attendant engaged in a serious conversation with a group of men in business suits about a conference presentation they were scheduled to deliver. She managed to be just the right flight attendant for each passenger.

A week later, on our return flight, lo and behold, Andrade happened to be working again. Smiling, we said hello, not knowing if she'd remember us. She beamed at us and replied, this time in Hebrew, "An *entire* can!"

The plane was nearly empty, so we had a chance to talk with Andrade at greater length. We learned that she was born in Argentina, the fifth of eight children. "There's so many of us siblings," she said, "that I'm always on the phone with someone from my family. At least once a day."

We assumed she'd learned Hebrew in school or from relatives, but it turned out she'd picked it up on a two-week trip to Israel she took with a friend on a whim twenty years ago. She is fluent in Spanish, English, French, Italian, and Portuguese. But she also knows key phrases in many other languages: German, Japanese, Hebrew, Arabic. "I can ask you, 'How are you?' in English," she told us, "and you will answer, but if I use your own language, something in you will shine from inside."

Andrade has a natural tendency to match her personality to the people she encounters and to figure out what will make *them* more comfortable. She's always been fascinated with people. She has had a variety of jobs, from working for Club Med to tutoring people in foreign languages to her current career as a flight attendant. "The magic of meeting new people is what feeds me."

Even in her free time Andrade finds creative ways to form emotional bonds with others. "I like to have garage sales," she told us, "not just to get rid of junk but also to connect with people. Someone might ask me how much I want for something. 'Name the price—I'll pay *you* to take it.' I like the spontaneity and the unexpected." Her approach and attitude make her stand out in people-oriented professions.

Maia Andrade is a natural at making people feel at ease while flying. Similarly, Dina Kaplan loves interacting with customers and investors alike. But how well do such traits translate to more formal corporate environments?

To find the answer, Cambridge professor Martin Kilduff and David Day of Pennsylvania State University studied MBA students as they were starting their round of on-campus job interviews. On average, a student signed up for sixteen interviews and chose among three job offers. These are very motivated individuals about to embark on careers in banking, consulting, and management—jobs in rather buttoned-down companies and institutions. The researchers asked each student to complete a questionnaire on self-monitoring. Kilduff and Day continued to follow the students after they left school to begin their jobs, by analyzing data from the alumni center and tracking the career moves of each alumnus.

Kilduff and Day uncovered a pattern that, at first glance, seemed to contradict the notion of the high self-monitor as someone who is adaptable and likable. The high self-monitoring MBA grads were much more likely to bounce around from job to job and move from company to company. If high self-monitors were so good at forming relationships, why did they keep switching jobs?

As it turned out, the high self-monitors weren't having problems in the workplace. Quite the opposite: as a group, they were far more likely to win promotions at other companies than were their lower-self-monitoring counterparts. And because high self-monitors are so adaptable, they were more willing to make the move to a different company. As a result, they were able to progress much further in their careers than were the rest of their classmates. "Being able to adapt their behavior to circumstances," explained Kilduff and Day, "and being ready to follow opportunity to another employer . . . may have helped the high self-monitors get ahead." Even those high self-monitors who stayed at the same company for years, Kilduff and Day discovered, received more promotions within their companies than their fellow alumni. It was clear that high self-monitors were doing *something* differently from everyone else that made them very successful in their careers.

Remember the Brazilian model who seemed to click with everyone at Elite? She was joining one of the most competitive agencies in the world during the busiest and most hectic time of year. Before she arrived, as far as the staff at Elite were concerned, she was just another young model trying to make it. If we were in her shoes, most of us would try to make a good impression, smile, shake a few people's hands. But the Brazilian model was incredibly fluid in her approach. She didn't just fit in but got noticed by the head of the agency himself, a guy who was so overwhelmed by interruptions and intrusions that day that he was literally hiding from his staff.

It's a pattern that Martin Kilduff, working with another research team, was able to identify in one high self-monitor after another. Because they were so fluid and adaptable, high self-monitors always seemed to end up at the center of any social network they encountered. And they were able to do so remarkably quickly.

Kilduff and his team interviewed the entire staff of a small technology company—a firm of approximately a hundred individuals—where they collected data about each person's self-monitoring tendencies. Later, they asked each employee a set of detailed questions about each of his or her coworkers. In other words, they didn't just have information about Tom and Mary; they now knew how each of Tom and Mary's coworkers perceived them. The team was able to create intricate relationship matrices—each matrix contained 10,302 unique data points. This gave Kilduff and the other researchers an objective map of which individuals were at the center of a particular social or professional network (as well as which individuals were more isolated).

Time after time, high self-monitors occupied the central spots within the networks: they were the intermediaries and conduits through whom information was conveyed and friendships were formed. They were the ones at the center of watercooler relationships, the ones assigned key roles within a team.

It was especially interesting just how quickly the high self-monitors were able to capture such central roles. If you look at a graph of a low-self-monitoring employee across time within the social dynamics of a company, you'll see a steady, linear progression; the longer he (or she) has been working for the company, the more deeply connected he becomes. After many years, after all, everyone comes to know you, you develop friendships, and people come to you for your experienced perspective.

Now let's look at another employee in a similar job, with similar skills and educational background, who has just joined the company. The only difference is that this employee happens to be a high self-monitor. If we were to chart her relationship matrix on the same graph, we would see a remarkable pattern. The slow-and-steady linear progression of the low self-monitoring employee is replaced by an explosive burst of social activity. In only eighteen months, a high self-monitor is able to achieve the same visibility and company-wide relationships that low self-monitors take more than thirteen years to develop. Before long, high self-monitors have a level of social and professional connection far surpassing that of even the most tenured low self-monitors.

Thirteen years versus a year and a half. Those who've spent time in the corporate world sometimes look at high self-monitors as employees who are more political than the average person. They assume that high self-monitors schmooze their way to the top, angling for the next promotion, always trying to gain an edge. It does, however, raise a natural question: do high self-monitors actively manipulate others—like used-car salesmen—to get people to like them?

Research psychologists Clara Michelle Cheng and Tanya Chartrand, from Ohio State University, decided to find out what the motivations of high self-monitors were. Are they genuine in their interactions, the researchers wondered, or do they just put on a show to advance their own interests? The problem, of course, is that one can't ask the high self-monitors outright—if they *are* naturally manipulative, they wouldn't give a straight answer. But Cheng and Chartrand found a clever way to measure authenticity without their subjects knowing that they were being monitored.

The researchers invited students from an introductory psychology class to participate in a study about how different individuals reacted to a varied collection of photographs. When each student arrived at the lab, he or she was told that another participant would be joining them shortly. This, of course, is where the real study began. A third of the students were told in advance that the other participant was a high school student. Another third were told that she was a graduate student. And the last third were told that the she was a classmate from Psych 100. In fact, the second participant was a fellow researcher, especially trained to elicit a mirroring response.

When the research accomplice came into the room, she adhered to a rehearsed script, which she repeated word for word in every single encounter. The script told her not only what to say but how to act. As the subject and the accomplice looked at and commented on different photos clipped from magazines—purportedly the real task of the experiment—the accomplice crossed her legs and gently shook her foot, the kind of nervous tic people sometimes exhibit in new situations. This foot shaking was the true crux of the experiment. Cheng and Chartrand wanted to know if the subjects would mirror the researcher and start shaking their feet as well.

The researchers found that most people seemed to take no notice—their own behavior didn't change at all. On average, the subjects shook their feet during only 1 to 2 percent of the time they spent with the accomplice. They acted no differently whether they thought the fellow participant was a classmate, a grad student, or a high school student.

The reaction by those who were high self-monitors, though, was not as clear-cut. When the high self monitors believed that the researcher was a high school student or a graduate student, their own foot-shaking behavior was minimal, essentially the same rate as that of everyone else. But when the high-self-monitoring subjects thought that the accomplice was a classmate, their foot shaking spiked, increasing nearly tenfold.

If the high self-monitors were being strategic, one would think they would have mirrored the grad student— who was ahead of them academically—rather than their classmate. But to the high-self-monitoring subjects, the fellow Psych 100 student was a peer and part of their cohort, as Cheng and Chartrand explained, "whereas the high school student and graduate student were people likely never to be encountered again." Moreover, the high self-monitors commenced their mirroring reaction without being conscious of it. They had no idea that they were being recorded. But intuitively, they picked up on social cues in an unconscious effort to establish rapport. In other words, high self-monitors were mirroring their peers without even realizing they were doing so.

So, yes, high self-monitors have a natural ability to gravitate toward the center of a social or business network. But their actions and behavior do not appear to be strategic. Rather, they thrive on social connections and tend to make them effortlessly. Establishing a genuine connection with others—clicking with them—"makes life really fun," reflects Dina Kaplan. "Because when you're traveling to a distant place, even if it was a few years earlier and even if it was once and you clicked with them, you have all these people sprinkled across the world. It can be the opportunity to get involved in nonprofits, to go on trips, to attend events or conferences they are organizing. It ends up leading to a lot of wonderful opportunities that enrich your life."

Perhaps there is something the rest of us can learn from Maia Andrade and Dina Kaplan. We're naturally drawn to people who mirror our emotional states. Perhaps mirroring the emotional states of others in key situations would help us to better connect with them. Even more important, Andrade and Kaplan instinctively know that there's tremendous power in the moment when quick-set intimacy is formed. That's because interactions in which we click don't just affect the strength of our relationship with the other person—they bring out the best in *us* as well.

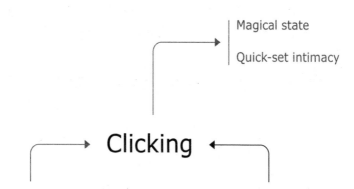

Magical state

Quick-set intimacy

Clicking

Click Accelerators

Vulnerability

Transactional
    Phatic
    Factual
    Evaluative

Connective
    Gut-level
    Peak

Proximity

Exponential Attraction
    Spontaneous communications
    Passive contacts

Resonance

Flow

Presence
    Intentionality
    Mutuality
    Individuality
    Attentiveness

Similarity

Quantity over quality

In-group

Long-lasting effect

Safe Place

Joint adversity

Frame

High Self-Monitors

Have fluid personalities

Modulate emotional expression

Quickly incorporate norms

Manage others' perceptions

Act as network hubs

CHAPTER 8

Personal Elevation

Peter Mathews, an unwieldy suitcase in one hand and a heavy notebook in the other, looked more like a hitchhiker on his way to a Grateful Dead concert than an anthropology student about to crack an ancient mystery. Right now, the long-haired, lanky twenty-one-year-old Australian was lost in the middle of the jungle in the Mexican state of Chiapas.

Only a month earlier, Peter had been at the university in Calgary, Canada, working feverishly on the notebook he was now clutching. If a casual reader were to look inside this notebook, all he or she would see was row upon row of three-digit numbers and pencil-drawn symbols. But to the trained eye, these numbers and images painted a cultural map of an entire civilization—a key to understanding the history of the region Peter was exploring.

As Peter trekked through the jungle, he knew that beneath the foliage and undergrowth surrounding him were majestic stone temples built by the ancient Maya around A.D. 600. Over the centuries, these once-grand structures had eroded and crumbled. But some important artifacts remained: limestone walls inscribed with Maya hieroglyphics. What was perplexing about the writing was that it was in a script long forgotten by the area's residents, descendants of the ancient Maya. Cryptologists from around the world had identified hundreds of unique characters, but despite decades of painstaking labor, they had come nowhere close to cracking the code.

All that was really understood about the texts was that there were some numbers, referring to calendar dates; a scattering of symbols, such as those for "sun," "moon," and "river"; and the occasional name of a Maya ruler. The generally accepted theory at the time held that the Maya texts were simply a loose collection of primitive drawings. After all, no other indigenous people on the American continent had developed a complete written language.

Anthropologists figured that the Maya were more or less following the rules of Pictionary. They had a spoken language, the reasoning went, and they used pictograms to convey basic thoughts—something along the lines of "Year 1108, lots of rain, food."

That's where Peter Mathews entered the story. For months he had been working on a special college project involving the painstaking task of identifying Maya hieroglyphs from detailed photos taken at a site called Palenque. Although not the largest Maya ruin site, Palenque was unique in that the carved stone had stayed remarkably well preserved over the ages and offered a nearly complete text to decipher.

Peter would stay up into the small hours of the night examining the Palenque glyphs, matching them to previously established catalog numbers. A small circle inscribed within a larger square, for example, was given the catalog number 511. A hieroglyph resembling an eagle wearing eyeglasses and a turban was number 750b, and so on. By the time he was done, Peter's notebook contained every date inscribed at Palenque, the associated glyphs, and notes detailing anything any other researchers had ever written about the meaning of those dates.

As fate would have it, just as Peter was finishing the cataloging, his college advisor received an unexpected invitation to attend a conference in Palenque. The conference host, a woman named Merle Robertson, was an enthusiast who had become fascinated with the Maya site. She had opened her private home to host the conference near the location in the jungle where the Maya ruins lay. Peter's advisor couldn't attend because he was heading out on sabbatical. Eventually the department decided to send Peter in his stead.

That's how, on this December day, fourteen hundred years after the temple's heyday, Peter found himself in the Chiapas jungle, struggling to make his way to Palenque.

"As I walked down the dirt road," Peter told us years later, "I wasn't quite sure where I was or even where Merle Robertson's house was." Suddenly Peter heard a woman shouting his name: "Peter? Peter! Are you Peter Mathews?" The only person who could possibly know who he was, he thought, was Merle Robertson. But when he asked the woman if she was Merle, she retorted, "Hell no, I'm Linda Schele."

Linda Schele, the granddaughter of a Tennessee moonshiner, had arrived in Palenque years earlier on an impromptu Christmas trip to Mexico to study Maya art. Boisterous and outgoing, with a penchant for salty language, Linda was informal in her demeanor and as impulsive as Peter Mathews was meticulous. Two years ago, she and her husband had decided to take a detour and visit the Palenque ruins. An art teacher by profession, Linda was intrigued by the elaborate Maya glyphs; what was intended to be a two-hour visit turned into a substantially longer venture. "We stayed there for twelve days, until my students and David, my husband, got angry that we hadn't fulfilled our plans," Linda would later recall. "Against my grudging agreement, we went to Yucatán and spent twenty-four hours and came right back to Palenque." She continued to return to the site over the next two years.

When the two had finally sorted out who was who, Peter brought his suitcase inside and he and Linda started talking. "She was terribly gregarious," Peter remembers, "just filled with enthusiasm about whatever topic you were discussing at the time."

Their conversation quickly turned to the writing on the temples. From the beginning, Peter and Linda seemed to feed off each other's enthusiasm for Maya glyphs. They felt an instant attraction to each other, although their relationship was never romantic. "We just got on like hell and fire. Her enthusiasm was very infectious. I can't explain it," reflected Peter, "other than to say we clicked."

Over the course of the next couple of days at Palenque, Peter and Linda spent most of their time together. When Linda offered to serve as a guide through the archeological site, Peter jumped at her offer. "We had a wonderful time walking around the ruins," Peter recalled. "I think this is when I really knew I found my vocation."

Through the lens of what we've learned up to this point about clicking, we can see a whole host of forces conspiring to bring Peter Mathews and Linda Schele together. In a photograph taken of the conference attendees, Peter and Linda stand out visibly as the youngest. They also shared a passion for deciphering the Maya writings. Predisposed to be attracted to each other as friends, they spent hours together in close proximity, either in Merle Robertson's house or walking in the jungle. And the conference environment itself created a clearly delineated community that helped to bring Peter and Linda together.

We've already seen how such forces foster and accelerate clicking. We've looked at how we feel about others when we click with them and how others, in turn, feel about us. Now we turn our attention to how we *change* as a result of the interaction.

In Rom's study about magical experiences, time and again participants remembered feeling a sense of euphoria. In the magic of the moment, we tend to see the person with whom we click in the best possible light. He or she, in turn, sees us in a similar light, and being seen that way makes a world of difference.

Perhaps in response to the intense emotional connection we make, when we click we tend to become our best selves. That doesn't mean just being nice or charming with this new person in our lives. We also become more open, more creative, more willing to stretch ourselves beyond our comfort zone. This may be why so many of us are drawn to quick-set intimacy. Not only do we experience the intensity of the connection, but we experience *ourselves* in a different, better way.

On the afternoon of the last day of the conference in Palenque, the rest of the attendees decided to explore Mexico before heading home. "Most of the conference attendees were going to nearby sites or just relaxing," remembers Peter. "But Linda and I decided to get out the notebook I had brought with me, with all the dates and symbols, and play around with it."

Up to this point, the anthropological community had thought that the approximately eight hundred Maya hieroglyphs symbolized basic, fundamental concepts. Peter and Linda were about to shatter that theory. Peter recalled how their discovery unfolded: "We put all the date glyphs in chronological order. We weren't afraid at all to be wrong. We'd throw ideas out and test them and move on from there." Writing on large pieces of blank chart paper, the two arranged and rearranged the few strands of text that had already been deciphered, trying to see if they could glean any more clues about the nature of the complete text.

Experts, of course, had been trying to crack the Maya glyphs for decades. Peter, a twenty-one-year-old undergrad with no experience in cryptology, and Linda, an art teacher who had happened on the site during a vacation, really had no business even attempting to tackle a puzzle like this one. But they were about to experience the benefits of personal elevation.

As the conference's afternoon break was drawing to a close, Peter and Linda took a closer look at excerpts where calendar dates happened to be written in close proximity to glyphs associated with rulers' names. They took the segments and laid them all out on one of the big sheets. "We were just playing with it, seeing what would happen. All of a sudden, we saw the pattern fall before our eyes. After four or five dates, it became quite clear."

Here was what their list looked like, with the Maya dates converted into today's modern Gregorian calendar:

Ruler Name	Associated Dates
Lord Shield Pacal	March 23, 603
	July 29, 615
	August 28, 683
	68 years, 33 days

Lord Chan-Bahlum	May 23, 635
	January 10, 684
	February 20, 702
	18 years, 40 days
Lord Hok	November 5, 644
	May 30, 702
	August [illegible], 720
	18 years, 72 days
Lord Chaac	September 13, 678
	[illegible]
	December 30, 721
	[illegible]
Lord Chac-Zutz	January 23, 671
	June 17, 723
	August 20, 731
	8 years, 64 days

Although a few of the dates are missing, the meaning of the dates starts to emerge when you consider them in relation to one another. Take a look, for example, at the third date associated with Lord Shield Pacal: August 28, 683. It closely follows the second date associated with Lord Chan-Bahlum: January 10, 684. What Peter and Linda realized was that the second date referred to the time when the ruler took power. And the time span referred to the period of time each of the rulers reigned.

Look at the third date associated with a ruler and compare it with the second date of the next ruler, and notice how close together they are:

August 28, 683	January 10, 684
February 20, 702	May 30, 702
August [illegible], 720	[illegible]
December 30, 721	June 17, 723

In each case, these two dates are separated by a period of mere months. Linda and Peter realized this couldn't be a coincidence. One of the most important days in a ruler's life is the day he takes power, which naturally occurs relatively soon after the death of his predecessor. They concluded that the second date was the day the ruler ascended the throne, and the third date marked his death. Lord Shield Pacal died on August 28, 683; his successor, Lord Chan-Bahlum, took the reins a few months later, on January 10, 684. The first date, Peter and Linda reasoned, must be the ruler's birth.

Looking at the dates associated with Lord Shield Pacal, who for years had been known only by an abstract-seeming symbol, Peter and Linda realized that he was born in 603, took the throne when he was twelve, and died when he was eighty. A few months later, his successor, forty-eight-year-old Lord Chan-Bahlum, rose to power. When Chan-Bahlum died, his successor, Lord Hok, became ruler at age fifty-seven, and so on. Putting the remaining pieces of the puzzle together, simple math revealed that the fourth lines (e.g., "68 years, 33 days") were an exact calculation of each ruler's time in power.

Peter and Linda's breakthrough revealed that the written Maya language was anything but primitive. The Palenque glyphs recorded a running history of the Maya people. Indeed, when the other glyphs were incorporated into the interpretation, they revealed a complex and complete narrative. In the course of a couple of hours, Peter and Linda had accomplished what the experts had failed to achieve in decades.

"The final day, the final three hours of that conference," reflected Linda, " . . . all of a sudden, we broke two hundred years of history and found the names of eight kings. It's like the Rosetta Stone and going to the moon and all of that happening in three hours. It was one of those magic, almost unrepeatable [moments]."

Thirty years later, Peter, now a professor of archaeology at La Trobe University in Australia, tried to reconstruct the events leading up to the Palenque breakthrough. He saw a direct connection between the discovery and the intense chemistry between him and Linda. "One of the triggers for our collaboration," Peter told us, "was that we got along so well that we could suspend our own personalities to a degree. Intellectually, we could suspend the normal kinds of checks and balances that you might have in an enterprise like this. Linda provided that spark; we were able to bring all of our individual knowledge into practical use." His recollection offers an insider's perspective on personal elevation in action.

Researchers from Northwestern's Kellogg Graduate School of Management and the University of Pennsylvania's Wharton School, seeking to measure the effect of personal elevation, studied first-year MBA students in the midst of their "core" courses in accounting, finance, operations, and statistical analysis. The students took these classes with the same relatively small cohort. And as is the case within any group, people in the class were more naturally drawn to certain classmates than to others.

The researchers selected a representative group of students from among the first-year MBAs and asked them to list up to ten classmates they felt closest to and most comfortable with. In other words, they were asked to identify the people they clicked with the most. After the researchers collected and analyzed the questionnaires, the students were told they would be divided into three-person teams. What the students didn't know was that half of the teams were composed entirely of individuals who clicked with one another (that is, every person on the team had listed every other person on the team as someone with whom they clicked), while the other half of the teams were composed of people who were classmates but who didn't click.

The triads were then asked to perform two activities

that had nothing to do with calculators, spreadsheets, or anything else an MBA student would encounter on a daily basis. The idea was to start with a blank slate. For the first activity, each team was seated around a table piled high with Tinkertoys, straws, wooden sticks, and macaroni. The students were told to use the arts-and-crafts materials in front of them to construct three-dimensional abstract models (such as two cubes and a pyramid, or a tall cylinder surrounded by blocks) based on a blueprint that was provided.

After conveying the instructions and making sure the students understood what was expected of them, the researchers got out of the way and left the teams to work through the task on their own. They returned after the task was completed to assess the accuracy and speed with which each group had performed it.

When the students had completed the construction project, they were given a more intellectually challenging task. Teams were given a stack of folders, each containing the business school application materials—résumé, essays, transcript, and recommendation letters—of several business school applicants. The students were told to carefully evaluate the application packages and rank the candidates on six separate scales: academic abilities, interpersonal skills, focus, motivation, career progress, and outside activities. After considering each applicant, the team had to come up with an "accept," "reject," or "wait-list" decision.

The researchers then compared these decisions against the decisions arrived at by the school's admissions committee.

When the researchers evaluated the teams' performances against an objective scale, it turned out that, on both tasks, the teams made up of students who clicked performed better than the groups made up of students who didn't click. But what was surprising was the *magnitude* by which the teams of students who clicked had outperformed their non-clicking counterparts. They successfully constructed 20 percent more models than the mere-acquaintance triads and were 70 percent more accurate on the admissions evaluations.

Was this the result of personal elevation? To answer this question, the researchers placed recording devices that captured exactly what was being said among each of the teams. Listening to the conversations, the researchers formed a blow-by-blow picture of just how quick-set intimacy affects interpersonal interactions. The recordings revealed that the team members who didn't click were, by and large, quite cordial with one another but more or less went through the motions in following the instructions they were given. Think of being placed on a team with colleagues with whom you don't necessarily have any personal spark. You'd do your best to just get along and accomplish the task at hand.

By contrast, the teams made up of students who clicked exhibited a markedly increased level of energy and enthusiasm in tackling each task. In the first exercise, where the teams were given a menial and not particularly stimulating assignment, the teams made up of students who clicked were three times more likely to cheer one another on. If you listened in on the teams whose members didn't click, not surprisingly, they sounded like students being forced to construct silly, boring models. The teams whose members clicked, in comparison, sounded like fans cheering on their team during the homecoming game.

When it came to the admissions task, the teams made up of students that clicked were much more focused and hardworking than their counterparts. The task was designed to elicit conflict—it was unlikely that all three people would share the same view on an admissions decision. The teams made up of students who didn't click had little conflict; instead, they opted to reach an admissions decision that no one was particularly happy with but that at least enabled the group to move on. The teams made up of students who clicked, on the other hand, actually entered into conflict—but a healthy conflict based on the task content, not on each other. "High performance on the [admissions] decision-making task," the researchers found, "was attributed to low levels of emotional and administrative conflict and high levels of task content conflict." That is, the conflict was intellectually spirited and passionate but never became personal.

When we interact with people with whom we've formed an instant connection, we tend to give each other the benefit of the doubt. The trust that forms gives us permission to disagree, because we know that our counterpart will support us emotionally, even if we diverge in our opinions.

Looking at the two tasks together, it's clear that the teams made up of students who clicked brought more gusto and energy to their projects. They saw the best in one another. They cheered one another on when they needed encouragement and were comfortable confronting one another when the task required mental acuity. They were more willing to go beyond their individual comfort zones.

In the work world, this is a crucial point. When assigning project teams, it's tempting to keep relationships professional and separate business from pleasure. But those individuals who click, who have a natural connection with one another, are more likely to form a productive team. Those teams succeed not just because they get along but because of how they function when they don't agree.

Business professors Keith Murnighan and Donald Conlon studied the organizational dynamics of string quartets to find out why some quartets are successful and others aren't. When you watch a highly skilled string quartet in a concert hall, it's easy to forget that these talented musicians are ordinary people who, like many of us, have to learn how to make a small team work. The first violinist in a string quartet is often the face of the ensemble. He or she must be a strong performer, but not someone who stands so far above everyone else as to overshadow the rest of the group. The second violinist supports and harmonizes with the first violinist, while successfully blending in with the others. The violinist and cellist must strike similar balances. Imagine how challenging it is to spend as many as six hours a day, seven days a week, with the same three other musicians, in a small room, making minute adjustments in performance and navigating each person's personality quirks.

Because there is no conductor, the performers have to resolve any issues that arise among themselves and decide together what particular interpretation to give to a piece. "Any composition can be played an infinite number of ways, with varying speed, emphasis, rhythm, balance, and phrasing," explain Murnighan and Conlon. In preparing to perform a piece, a quartet develops its own unique style. "A quartet tries to stamp each performance with its own character."

Murnighan and Conlon evaluated a number of ensembles and collected data about their concert fees, their album sales, the number of concerts they had performed over the previous year, the number of newspaper and magazine reviews they had garnered in a given six-month period, and the mean ratings of the abstracted reviews. The researchers found that the quartets fell at either extreme of a spectrum. At one end there were a number of very successful quartets that got the lion's share of the press reviews, gigs, and recording contracts. At the other extreme were quartets that were just barely getting by. The surprising thing was that there weren't any professional quartets that were somewhere in between, enjoying a moderate level of success. For string quartets, either you're a rock star, so to speak, or you're playing gigs at weddings and bars. You're either flourishing or just scraping by.

The most obvious-seeming explanation for the disparity was that the more successful ensembles were simply composed of better musicians who possessed more musical ability, experience, training, or raw talent. But just as in the elite modeling world, where beauty is a prerequisite, all the performers in any professional string quartet were basically at the very top of their field. The musicians were equally proficient, well trained, and talented.

The real reason for the success of some quartets, in fact, had little to do with musical ability. After conducting in-depth interviews with the musicians in the ensembles, the researchers sat in on practice sessions and carefully observed any differences among the groups. It turned out that the biggest differentiator between successful and unsuccessful ensembles was the dynamics of each group. The successful quartets, at the core of things, clicked, much like Peter Mathews and Linda Schele. The less successful quartets conducted themselves in a "strictly business," professional manner—the musicians respected one another but didn't have a close rapport. When the researchers matched up the group dynamics with the quartets' success, they found that the quartets made up of musicians that clicked significantly outperformed their strictly business counterparts. The difference is noteworthy: quartets in which the musicians clicked produced dozens of albums, as opposed to a handful by the strictly business quartets; they charged twice as much in concert fees; and they received five times the reviews.

When it came down to it, the members of the successful quartets interacted with one another in much the same way that the MBA students who clicked interacted in their three-person teams. Members of these quartets were more supportive of one another and more likely to cheer one another on. When tough decisions had to be made, they weren't afraid to confront one another, and conflict was dealt with in a healthy manner that focused on the issues at hand rather than on interpersonal bickering.

The businesslike quartets remained cordial and let conflict roll off their backs. They spent *less* time arguing than their counterparts. But in truth, each member remained more resentful that his or her vision for interpreting a given piece wasn't being listened to or accepted by the group. So although the quartets played well in rehearsal, when it came time for the performance, each member tended to revert back to how he or she had interpreted the piece in the first place. The resulting sound just wasn't as cohesive or polished to the audience, which voted in concert ticket and album purchases.

Ultimately, the way people in a group click can make a measurable difference in their success, whether they are MBA students participating in an experiment or a musical ensemble performing before the public. The passion, energy, sheer joy, and enthusiasm the members of such groups experience help to bring out their best selves.

Peter Mathews and Linda Schele continued to collaborate and stay in close touch over the years following their breakthrough. In 1997 Linda was diagnosed with pancreatic cancer; she knew she had only a few months to live. "The thing that really amazed me," Peter told us, "was toward the end of Linda's life, when I was in her house in Texas. We were looking something up. We started talking about it at ten o'clock at night. And at three in the morning we were still talking about it. We lost all sense of time. And we were just enthusiastically going down the path of checking out what it was we were looking at. We both said at the same time, 'Gee, this is just like the old times in Palenque.' We both realized at the same time that the spark was still there, that every time we got together it was like this. And how wonderful that was . . . We both felt blessed. It's an amazing gift."

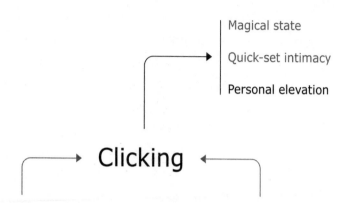

Clicking

Click Accelerators

Vulnerability

  Transactional
    Phatic
    Factual
    Evaluative

  Connective
    Gut-level
    Peak

Proximity

  Exponential Attraction
    Spontaneous communications
    Passive contacts

Resonance

  Flow

  Presence
    Intentionality
    Mutuality
    Individuality
    Attentiveness

Similarity

  Quantity over quality
  In-group
  Long-lasting effect

Safe Place

  Joint adversity
  Frame

High Self-Monitors

Have fluid personalities

Modulate emotional expression

Quickly incorporate norms

Manage others' perceptions

Act as network hubs

Magical state

Quick-set intimacy

Personal elevation

Conclusion: Bringing It All Together

There's a photograph of the two of us in our family album: Rom is a toddler and Ori is barely old enough to sit upright. Ori, with a full head of blond hair, is sitting in front of a campfire looking straight ahead, and Rom, dressed in bell-bottom corduroys, is approaching him from the side, planting a big kiss on his cheek.

We weren't asked to pose for the camera. It was a spontaneous moment captured on film that encapsulates the relationship we had growing up. It's not that we never fought or argued. Like all siblings, we had our moments. But when it came down to it—after we'd finally decided who deserved that last piece of candy or whose turn it was to take out the garbage—we were there for each other.

That connection followed us throughout our lives. To this day, whenever we're not quite sure about a decision—ranging from what vacation package to book to which family recipe to follow or what mutual fund to choose—we turn to each other. Maybe it's because we have such a long history together or because we think alike, but we've grown to depend on that connection. It's what sparked our interest in human connections and the phenomenon of clicking in the first place. The challenge in this pursuit, of course, was that no university has a department that we could contact for information. There are no conventions about the topic that we could attend. But as the previous chapters have demonstrated, the way that people click with others and with the world around them is such a central part of the human condition that it comes up in one way or another in a wide variety of fields and activities, from romantic relationships to corporate work teams, from analyses of neurobiological brain activity patterns to studies on the relationship dynamics between absolute strangers.

We wanted to understand the building blocks of quickset intimacy—what the factors are that lead a person to click with someone else or become fully alive in a specific activity, from writing a novel to playing an instrument, from finding oneself "in the zone" in a pickup basketball game to gazing into your wife's eyes over a romantic dinner and feeling connected in the way you were when you first met. What causes people to be fully engaged with the world around them? The most rewarding part of our research has been hearing the stories of people who have clicked. You can see the excitement in their eyes, the change in their voice as they tell you their story. In a way, we have been trying to understand the experience of clicking for much of our adult lives—from Rom's research with magical experiences to Ori's involvement with Touchy-Feely groups at Stanford.

In this book, we've explored clicking from a number of different perspectives—what happens when we click, how we form quick-set connections, and why these connections can affect our subsequent experiences and relationships years later. As a result of this journey, we've distilled what we have found to be the key aspects of clicking. They are summarized below.

1. **Magic matters.** We began by exploring the euphoric sensation we experience when we click with another person or activity and how the pleasure center in our brain rewards us when we make such a connection. Indeed, many of the people we interviewed described clicking as having a magical quality. Most of us assume such moments happen only serendipitously. We are unaware of our ability to help foster or create such moments in our lives.

2. **There's power in vulnerability.** Most of us are reluctant to open up and disclose personal information to others. We fear coming across as needy, unprofessional, or overly emotional. But our willingness to risk being vulnerable can deepen the quality of our relationships and make us *more* likely to connect with others. Most of our verbal interactions with others take place on a transactional level (a level that conveys only

basic information). As a result, we routinely miss out on opportunities to communicate on a connective, emotional level. By paying close attention to the way we communicate, we can actively shift the degree to which we open up to others and communicate that we're open to connecting more fully with them.

3. **A few feet make a big difference.** Simply put, even the smallest distances that separate us from others play a major role in determining who we're most likely to hit it off with. In a concession to efficiency and multitasking, it's tempting to avoid meetings and face-to-face interactions. But what we don't take into account is that we're missing opportunities to get closer to the people we work and interact with.

4. **Resonance begets resonance.** Flow—the experience of being in the zone—and being fully present help us to create resonance, a quality that can draw others to us. It makes sense to strive to be fully present with the people around us, paying close attention to what they say and do, their attitudes and their needs. As you reach out to them, take their emotional temperature.

5. **Similarity counts; quantity trumps quality.** It doesn't really matter whether we share a first name, a birthday, a home state, or a rare fingerprint pattern—similarity can help to create an in-group dynamic that brings people together. The more we can zero in on and accentuate the similarities we have with someone else, the more likely we are to hit it off with that person.

This is especially useful in trying to connect with someone who seems very different from us. If the person is from a different cultural background or a different profession or industry, focus on the ways in which you are similar—music, sports, humor. You're more likely to create a connection.

6. **The environment around us can help foster intimacy.** Certain surroundings and situations nurture quick-set intimacy. Overcoming challenges or adversity together can help to stimulate or encourage clicking, as can being part of a shared, defined community.

7. **Certain people are magnets.** As we've seen, some people are more naturally prone to clicking than others. High self-monitors instinctively modulate their emotions to match and meet others emotionally. What can we learn from them? The more aware you are of the other person's mind-set, attitude, and emotions, the better your likelihood of being able to connect with him or her.

8. **Quick-set intimacy can bring out the best in us.** Being around others with whom we click can spur us to perform at a higher level. We're more comfortable, more willing to be ourselves, more willing to be open and express disagreement in a way that can be worked out in a healthy and productive fashion.

It's unfortunate that the magic of quick-set intimacy is usually left to chance and serendipity. As we've seen, we can help to foster those times when we click with our colleagues, potential romantic partners, and the world around us. And when we do, that connection can be, well, magical. It can change the very nature of a relationship—not just at that moment but forever after. It can help us to achieve our best selves.

ACKNOWLEDGMENTS

I s it any surprise that many of the people mentioned in this section are also individuals with whom we instantly clicked?

Our wives, naturally, come to mind. Hilary Roberts has continued to inject elegance into our writing, and Josyn Herce elegance into everything visual. We're grateful for the continual support of our parents, Tsilla and Hagay Brafman.

Our superb agent, Esther Newberg—another instant connection—has remained a steadfast supporter and keen advisor, and we are also continually grateful to have ICM's Liz Farrell and Kari Stuart on our team.

Roger Scholl's enthusiasm and insight have made him an invaluable partner in the creation of this book. It has been a true pleasure working with everyone at Broadway Books. We especially appreciate Michael Palgon for his vision and guidance, Meredith McGinnis for her creativity, Tara Gilbride for championing the book, Talia Krohn for her thoughtful feedback, Anna Thompson for keeping the process on track, Sarah Rainone for her belief in our ideas, and Liz Hazelton, who has been with us from the very start.

We feel fortunate to have had the opportunity to hear many people's most meaningful and special life stories. Huge thanks to Paul and Nadia Butler, Jim West, Gerhard Sessler, Greg Sancier, Bob Scigalski, Michael Ellsberg, Mike Welch, Fred Berner, Liz Manne, Mario Andretti, Patty Reid, Klaus Meine, Lidia Bastianich, Kelly Hildebrandt and Kelly Hildebrandt, Donn Byrne, Fred Wahpepah, John Karren, Dina Kaplan, Neal Hamil, Maia Andrade, Chris Constable, Peter Mathews, Cynthia Cohen, Laurie Davis, and Ben Karney.

Some of the first eyes on this manuscript were those of Steven Rotkoff, Alison Roberts, Denise Egri, and Colin Bach; we thank them for their meticulous reading and feedback. Ever since we first shared the concept for the book, Mark Fortier has provided valuable input, and his passion remains, as always, contagious.

Throughout the writing process, we've been bolstered by the support of family and friends: Nira Chaikin, Sarah'le Zerkov, Megan and John Hutchinson, David Blatte, Michael Breyer, Chip Conley, Martin Dempsey and TRADOC, Franz Epting, Tim Ferriss, Gabrielle Fishman, Marco Gemignani, Richie Hecker, Adam Hirsch, Bob Jesse, Noah Kagan, Matt Miller and Katie Brown, Corey Modeste, Aviva Mohilner, Liz O'Donnell, Sara Olsen, Pablo Pazmino, Ryan and Alexis Pickrell, Amy Pillitteri, Judah and the Pollacks, Juliette

Powell, Seth Roberts, Josh Rosenblum, Craig Sakowitz, Mark Schlosberg, Annie Shiau, Shams Shirley, Amy Shuster, Pete Sims, Rudy Tan, Astro Teller, Pam and Roy Webb, Kimberly Wicoff, Rene Wong, Cort Worthington, and so many others. We're fortunate to have you in our lives.

Ori and Rom are often asked to speak in person about topics related to their writing, and they enjoy the experience of reaching out and connecting with their audiences. They have spoken in front of diverse audiences, including Fortune 500 companies, businesses, university students, nonprofits, governmental organizations, and international conferences.

For more information, visit brafmanbrothers.com.

NOTES

8 **The two spent hours discussing science:** Jim West and Gerhard Sessler were inducted into the National Inventors Hall of Fame in 1999 for their 1962 invention of the modern electret microphone. They both continue to actively contribute to the acoustics research field and attend conferences together.

9 **Neuroscientists decided to try:** Arthur Aron, Helen Fisher, Debra J. Mashek, Greg Strong, Haifang Li, and Lucy L. Brown conducted the neurobiological research on individuals who reported feeling "madly in love." Their article, "Reward, Motivation, and Emotion Systems Associated with Early-Stage Intense Romantic Love," was published in the *Journal of Neurophysiology* 94 (2005): 327–37.

10 **To study this effect, neuroscientists:** The fMRI social outcast study examining the similarity between the neurological processing of physical and social pain is titled "Does Rejection Hurt? An fMRI Study of Social Exclusion" and was authored by Naomi I. Eisenberger, Matthew D. Lieberman, and

Kipling D. Williams. It was published in *Science* 302 (2003): 290–92.

12 **To answer these questions:** Rom's study about the magical quality of memorable connections is titled "The Living Experience of Magical Moments," Ph.D. dissertation, University of Florida, 2005.

16 **In the Netherlands, a husband-and-wife psychology team:** Husband-and-wife team Dick P. H. Barelds and Pieternel Barelds-Dijkstra explored relationship satisfaction levels among couples who began their relationship by either clicking, dating first, or starting out as friends. Their article is titled "Love at First Sight or Friends First? Ties Among Partner Personality Trait Similarity, Relationship Onset, Relationship Quality, and Love" and was published in the *Journal of Social and Personal Relationships* 24 (2007): 479–96.

CHAPTER 2: THE VULNERABLE HOSTAGE NEGOTIATOR AND THE CLICK ACCELERATORS

27 **As Sancier drove to the scene:** The name of the suspect with whom Officer Gregory Sancier performed the negotiations has been changed to ensure anonymity.

28 **In one study, individuals were brought into a room:** Judee K. Burgoon, Joseph B. Walther, and E. James Baesler conducted the brief touch experiment, titled "Interpretations, Evaluations, and Consequences of Interpersonal Touch," published in *Human Communication Research* 19 (1992): 237–63.

29 **During a job interview, for instance:** The effect of eye contact on hiring practices was examined in "Effects of Gaze on Hiring, Credibility, Attraction and Relational Message Interpretation," authored by Judee K. Burgoon, Valerie Manusov, Paul Mineo, and Jerold L. Hale. It was published in the *Journal of Nonverbal Behavior* 9 (1985): 133–46.

29 **Is there any truth to these sentiments?:** Recent studies have investigated the role of pheromones in physical attraction. Because of the subtle nature of the effect, scientists are still trying to fully understand the circumstances under which pheromones are most likely to play a significant role. The study described in the chapter is titled "Effects of Putative Male Pheromones on Female Ratings of Male Attractiveness: Influence of Oral Contraceptives and the Menstrual Cycle." It was written by Frances Thorne, Andrew Scholey, Mark Moss, and Bernhard Fink and published in *Neuroendocrinology Letters* 23 (2002): 291–97.

32 **The first accelerator, *vulnerability*:** Psychologist Sidney Jourard was the first person to scientifically examine the role of vulnerability through self-disclosure in interpersonal relationships. Jourard believed that self-disclosure is an essential ingredient in establishing intimacy. He also theorized that psychotherapists who appropriately disclose information about themselves help to form a more powerful healing relationship with their clients.

38 **At one end of the vulnerability spectrum:** Further information about the five levels of communication can be found

in John Powell's *Why Am I Afraid to Tell You Who I Am?* (Niles, IL: Argus Communications, 1969).

41 **It's a problem that social psychologist:** Arthur Aron, Edward Melinat, Elaine N. Aron, Robert Darrin Vallone, and Renee J. Bator paired up participants to study the effects of meaningful self-disclosure on clicking. Their study is called "The Experimental Generation of Interpersonal Closeness: A Procedure and Some Preliminary Findings." It was published in *Personality and Social Psychology Bulletin* 23 (1997): 363–77.

44 **Researcher Susan Singer Hendrick:** To learn more about how self-disclosure affects romantic relationships, see the following studies discussed in this section: "Self-Disclosure and Marital Satisfaction" by Susan Singer Hendrick, published in the *Journal of Personality and Social Psychology* 40 (1981): 1150–9; "Sexual Satisfaction and Sexual Self-Disclosure Within Dating Relationships," by E. Sandra Byers and Stephanie Demmons, published in the *Journal of Sex Research* 36 (1999): 180–89; and "Self-Presentation in Online Personals: The Role of Anticipated Future Interaction, Self-Disclosure, and Perceived Success in Internet Dating" by Jennifer L. Gibbs, Nicole B. Ellison, and Rebecca D. Heino, published in *Communication Research* 33 (2006): 152–77.

45 **Harvard Business School professor:** Youngme Moon, the Harvard professor who studied the effects of computer self-disclosure on students' engagement intimacy, described her results in an article titled "Intimate Exchanges: Using

Computers to Elicit Self-Disclosure from Consumers." *Journal of Consumer Research* 26 (2000): 323–39.

48 **Back in June 1992:** Further information about the 1992 Clinton campaign's decision to shift its tactics and the media analysts' reactions can be found in Christine F. Ridout's "News Coverage and Talk Shows in the 1992 Presidential Campaign," published in *Political Science and Politics* 26 (1993): 712–16. George Stephanopoulos wrote about his experience helping manage the Clinton campaign in "White House Confidential," *Newsweek* 129 (1997): 34. For a more elaborate analysis of the 1992 Clinton presidential campaign, we recommend *Covering Clinton: The President and the Press in the 1990s,* by Joseph Hayden (Westport, CT: Praeger, 2001).

CHAPTER 3: THE POWER OF PROXIMITY

55 **Four young sophomore players:** The stories of the oh-fours and their chemistry on and off the field can be found in "Florida Not Experiencing Any Sophomore Jinx," by Lee Jenkins, *New York Times,* March 26, 2006; "Go-Go Gators" by Grant Wahl, *Sports Illustrated,* April 10, 2006; and "Young Team a Surprise to Florida Coach, Too," Associated Press, March 20, 2006.

59 **A few weeks after completing their requirements:** Mady Wechsler Segal explored the effect of proximity on police cadets in the classroom in "Alphabet and Attraction: An Unobtrusive Measure of the Effect of Propinquity in a Field Setting," published in the *Journal of Personality and Social Psychology* 30 (1974): 654–57.

62 **The MIT apartments:** The MIT dorm study was conducted by Leon Festinger, Stanley Schachter, and Kurt W. Back. It is described in *Social Pressures in Informal Groups: A Study of Human Factors in Housing* (Stanford, CA: Stanford University Press, 1950).

65 **A study conducted by Bell Communications Research:** To learn more about the scientists' collaboration patterns as a function of distance, read "Patterns of Contact and Communication in Scientific Research Collaboration," by Robert Kraut, Carmen Egido, and Jolene Galegher, published in *Intellectual Teamwork: Social and Technological Foundations of Cooperative Work* (Hillsdale, NJ: Lawrence Erlbaum Associates, 1990), 149–71.

68 **To see the power of this kind of exchange:** The analysis of premeeting spontaneous conversations can be found in "Premeeting Talk: An Organizationally Crucial Form of Talk," by Julien C. Mirivel and Karen Tracy, published in *Research on Language and Social Interaction* 38 (2005): 1–34. We added punctuation to the transcribed dialogue for ease of reading.

71 **It's easier to gain an appreciation:** Pamela Hinds and Mark Mortensen conducted the study about the effect of proximity on working teams. It is described in "Understanding Conflict in Geographically Distributed Teams: The Moderating Effects of Shared Identity, Shared Context, and Spontaneous Communication," published in *Organization Science* 16 (2005): 290–307.

73 **Richard Moreland and Scott Beach:** Richard L. Moreland and Scott R. Beach wrote "Exposure Effects in the
Classroom: The Development of Affinity Among Students,"
describing the unconscious attraction that developed in students because of simple exposure. The article was published
in the *Journal of Experimental Social Psychology* 28 (1992):
255–76.

CHAPTER 4: WHEN EVERYTHING CLICKS

83 **In car racing, as in any other sport:** To learn more about
Mario Andretti's life and his passion for racing, we recom-
mend reading his autobiography, *What It's Like Out There*
(Chicago: Henry Regnery, 1970).

84 **Csikszentmihalyi wanted to identify the conditions:** Mihaly Csikszentmihalyi's book describing the state of flow is
aptly titled *Flow: The Psychology of Optional Experience* (New
York: HarperCollins, 1990). Csikszentmihalyi contends that
the experience of flow enriches our lives and makes us happier. Incidentally, the concept of flow is in some ways similar to Abraham Maslow's description of "peak experience,"
a psychological state wherein an individual experiences an
ecstatic, wonder-filled sensation that is distinctly different
from normal, everyday experience. Maslow, who was a pi-
oneer in the humanistic psychology movement, wanted to
move away from psychology's focus on pathology and study
the more positive aspects of living. Continuing the trend,
Csikszentmihalyi has been a champion of the positive psy-

chology movement, which seeks to empirically describe aspects of well-being.

86 **Jill Anderson, a nurse at Saint Alphonsus Regional Medical Center:** Jill Anderson's article on the importance of presence in nursing is titled "The Impact of Using Nursing Presence in a Community Heart Failure Program" and was published in the *Journal of Cardiovascular Nursing* 22 (2007): 89–94.

88 **Because presence plays such an important role:** An analysis of what it takes to be present can be found in Susan Tavernier's "An Evidence-Based Conceptual Analysis of Presence," published in *Holistic Nursing Practice* 20 (2006): 152–56.

89 **Interestingly, the power of presence lasts well beyond:** For more on the benefits of presence in the health care field, see "Nurses' Experiences of Being Present with a Patient Receiving a Diagnosis of Cancer," by Una Dunniece and Eamonn Slevin, published in the *Journal of Advanced Nursing* 32 (2000): 611–18.

93 **The contagiousness of resonance:** The research on mirror neurons is summarized in Giacomo Rizzolatti and Laila Craighero's "The Mirror-Neuron System," *Annual Review of Neuroscience*, 27 (2004): 169–92.

Chapter 5: The Seductive Power of Similarity

103 **Twenty-year-old Kelly Hildebrandt:** The story of the two Kelly Hildebrandts has received international media coverage in countries from Germany to Nigeria. The couple appeared

on NBC's *Today* show on July 19, 2009. The story and video are available at http://today.msnbc.msn.com/id/31994977.

105 **To better explain this, we'd like to introduce:** For Donn Byrne's entertaining description of his groundbreaking work on similarity, see "An Overview (and Underview) of Research and Theory Within the Attraction Paradigm," *Journal of Social and Personal Relationships* 14 (1997): 417–31.

112 **A team of psychologists from Santa Clara University:** The studies about the effect of perceived similarity (name, birthday, fingerprints) can be found in "What a Coincidence! The Effects of Incidental Similarity on Compliance," by Jerry M. Burger, Nicole Messian, Shebani Patel, Alicia del Prado, and Carmen Anderson. It was published in *Personality and Social Psychology Bulletin* 30 (2004): 35–43.

115 **Business professor J. Brock Smith of the University of Victoria:** J. Brock Smith's study on the effect of similarity on business relationships is described in "Buyer-Seller Relationships: Similarity, Relationship Management, and Quality," published in *Psychology & Marketing* 15 (1998): 3–21.

118 **Professor Avshalom Caspi, then at the University of Wisconsin–Madison:** The longitudinal study about the effect of similarity on relationship quality among married couples is titled "Shared Experiences and the Similarities of Personality: A Longitudinal Study of Married Couples." It was published in the *Journal of Personality and Social Psychology* 62 (1992): 281–91.

CHAPTER 6: FIRE, COMBAT, AND NATHAN'S LIVING ROOM:
THE ROLE OF PLACE

124 **Klerman and Weissman noticed an unusual phenomenon:** Gerald Klerman and Myrna Weissman's article on the rising rates of depression in industrialized countries is titled "Increasing Rates of Depression." It was published in the *Journal of the American Medical Association* 261 (1989): 2229–35.

126 **What had changed in Korea:** The story about the Korean sixth grader who used an online forum to seek guidance on how to commit suicide can be found in "Stress Brought On by Economic Growth Blamed for South Korea's Suicide Surge." It was written by Burt Herman and appeared in *USA Today* on February 10, 2007. You can find it at www.usatoday.com/news/health/2007–02–10-suicidesouthkorea_x.htm.

128 **A highly industrialized country such as Japan:** The Japanese study investigating the rates of depression between workers in traditional and modern occupations is "Relationship Between Diagnostic Subtypes of Depression and Occupation in Japan," by Koichiro Otsuka and Shigeaki Kato, published in *Psychopathology* 33 (2000): 324–28.

129 **Another person with small talk:** A good example (and one that inspired our thinking) of how joint adversity can foster connection can be found at www.blog.sethroberts.net/2009/09/20/how-to-talk-to-strangers/.

130 **John Karren, admissions director:** John Karren at Utah's Elements Wilderness Program explained to us that his organization takes a strength-based approach to empowering its

attendees and gets them to take ownership of their own lives and decisions.

131 **Sandra Jo Wilson and Mark W. Lipsey of Vanderbilt University pinpoint:** To learn more about the psychotherapeutic effects of wilderness camps, read "Wilderness Challenge Programs for Delinquent Youth: A Meta-analysis of Outcome Evaluations," by Sandra Jo Wilson and Mark W. Lipsey, published in *Evaluation and Program Planning* 23 (2000): 1–12.

131 **This concept of shared adversity:** The study about the Navajo sweat lodge for modern-day teenagers is "Using the Sweat Lodge Ceremony as Group Therapy for Youth," by Stephen Colmant and Rod Merta. It was published in the *Journal for Specialists in Group Work* 24 (1999): 55–73.

132 **A growing body of research suggests that:** Glen Elder and Elizabeth Clip authored "Wartime Losses and Social Bonding: Influences Across 40 Years in Men's Lives," published in *Psychiatry: Journal for the Study of Interpersonal Processes* 51 (1988): 177–98.

136 **The kibbutz movement in Israel:** You can find Naama Sabar's anthropological investigation, "Kibbutz LA: A Paradoxical Social Network," in the *Journal of Contemporary Ethnography* 31 (2002): 68–94.

142 **Those common bonds and that sense of community:** The study linking depression symptoms and the use of antidepressants with lack of workplace support is "Work Stress, Mental Health and Antidepressant Medication Findings from the Health 2000 Study," by Marianna Virtanen, Teija Honkonen, Mika Kivimaki, Kirsi Ahola, Jussi Vahtera, Arpo Aromaa, and

Jouko Lonnqvist. It was published in the *Journal of Affective Disorders* 98 (2007): 189–97.

CHAPTER 7: NATURALS

151 **Stanford University doctoral candidate:** Mark Snyder's pioneering work on self-monitoring is titled "Self-Monitoring of Expressive Behavior." It was published in the *Journal of Personality and Social Psychology* 30 (1974): 526–37.

156 **To find the answer:** The study that tracked MBAs in their new careers is titled "Do Chameleons Get Ahead? The Effects of Self-Monitoring on Managerial Careers." It was authored by Martin Kilduff and David Day and published in the *Academy of Management Journal* 37 (1994): 1047–60.

158 **It's a pattern that:** Ajay Mehra, Martin Kilduff, and Daniel Brass conducted a field study to measure the networking effects of high self-monitors in the workforce. See "The Social Networks of High and Low Self-Monitors: Implications for Workplace Performance," *Administrative Science Quarterly* 46 (2001): 121–46.

160 **Are they genuine in their interactions:** The creative study exploring the unconscious motivations of high self-monitors is titled "Self-Monitoring Without Awareness: Using Mimicry as a Nonconscious Affiliation Strategy." It was conducted by Clara Michelle Cheng and Tanya Chartrand and published in the *Journal of Personality and Social Psychology* 85 (2003): 1170–9.

Chapter 8: Personal Elevation

167 **As fate would have it:** To find out more about Peter Mathews and Linda Schele's story and the full history of how the Maya language was decoded, we recommend reading Michael Coe's *Breaking the Maya Code* (London: Thames and Hudson, 1993).

168 **Linda Schele, the granddaughter:** Andrew Weeks, Martin Simon, and Lori Conley produced a video recording of Linda Schele titled *Edgewalker: A Conversation with Linda Schele.* It was released in 1999 by Home Life Productions.

172 **Although a few of the dates are missing:** For more information about the chronology of the Maya decipherment, see *A Forest of Kings: The Untold Story of the Ancient Maya,* by David Freidel and Linda Schele (New York: Harper Perennial, 1992). Archaeologist Tatiana Proskouriakoff had independently found that some Maya hieroglyphs depicted dynastic time lines, but Peter and Linda were the first to show that the Maya written language was grammatically complex and completely corresponded to the Maya spoken language.

175 **The researchers collected a representative group of students:** Pri Pradhan Shah and Karen Jehn conducted the study about the MBAs who worked well as a team. Their work is titled "Do Friends Perform Better Than Acquaintances? The Interaction of Friendship, Conflict, and Task." It was published in *Group Decision and Negotiation* 2 (1993): 149–65.

179 **When you watch a highly skilled string quartet:** The investigation of group dynamics among string quartet members was authored by J. Keith Murnighan and Donald Conlon. It is titled "The Dynamics of Intense Work Groups: A Study of British String Quartets" and was published in *Administrative Science Quarterly* 36 (1991): 165–86.

INDEX